The RESOLVEDD Strategy of Ethical Decision Making

R eview of the details and background of the case

E stimate of the problem or conflict the case presents

S olutions reduced and grouped into a few main solutions

O utcomes of each main solution

L ikely impact of each main solution on people's lives

V alues upheld and violated by each main solution

E valuation of the values, outcomes, and likely impact of main solutions

D ecision stated, detailed, supported

D efense of the decision against objections to its main weaknesses

(See Checklist in Chapter 3.6.)

Ethics on the Job:
Cases and Strategies

❏ ❏ ❏ ❏ ❏ ❏ ❏

Ethics on the Job:
Cases and Strategies

❏ ❏ ❏ ❏ ❏ ❏ ❏

RAYMOND S. PFEIFFER
Delta College

RALPH P. FORSBERG
Delta College

Wadsworth Publishing Company
Belmont, California
A Division of Wadsworth, Inc.

Philosophy Editor: Kenneth King
Editorial Assistant: Gay Meixel
Production Editor: The Book Company
Print Buyer: Diana Spence
Designer: Kaelin Chappell
Copy Editor: Linda Purrington
Cover: Michael Rogondino
Signing Representative: Thor McMillen
Compositor: Bi-Comp., Inc.
Printer: Malloy Lithographing

This book is printed on acid-free paper that meets
Environmental Protection Agency standards for recycled
paper.

1 2 3 4 5 6 7 8 9 10—97 96 95 94 93

Library of Congress Cataloging-in-Publication Data

Pfeiffer, Raymond S.
    Ethics on the job : cases and strategies / Raymond
S. Peiffer, Ralph P. Forsberg.
        p.   cm.
    ISBN 0-534-19386-2
    1. Business ethics.   I. Forsberg, Ralph P.   II. Title.
HF5387.P45   1992
174'.4—dc20
                                                    92-21734
                                                    CIP

DEDICATION

❏ ❏ ❏ ❏ ❏ ❏ ❏

We dedicate this text to our mothers and fathers, who taught us that doing right is its own reward. And to LoLita, Sharon, Mariah, Ryan, Caven, and Darian, who taught us that when we are unsure of what is right, we must try harder to find out.

CONTENTS

❑ ❑ ❑ ❑ ❑ ❑ ❑

Cases: Personal Ethical Conflicts for Analysis 68

GUIDE TO TOPICS IN CASES

❏ ❏ ❏ ❏ ❏ ❏ ❏

PREFACE

❑ ❑ ❑ ❑ ❑ ❑ ❑

This is a text on practical ethics. Its purpose is to help the student master a clear, applicable strategy for making decisions in the presence of ethical conflict. It is not a text on theoretical ethics and does not provide a comprehensive treatment of the many concepts and issues in the field of ethics. However, neither does this book assume that the reader has general mastery of the subject of ethics. Many basic concepts needed to use the strategy are defined and exemplified in the text. The book is written for the general reader.

It is not the purpose of this book to persuade anyone of the importance of living an ethical life. Rather, the book assumes that the reader is already convinced of its importance, and is seeking ways to live accordingly. We have been impressed time and again by the comments of our students, friends, colleagues, associates, and acquaintances to the effect that they are unsure what is right and wrong in certain complex situations they encounter in their daily lives. Some have drawn the conclusion that there are no answers to such questions, or at least no best answers.

It is our conviction that many ambivalent situations do admit of better and worse determinations of what is right and wrong. Indeed, the confusion and frustration arising in many such situations seem to result more from someone's inability to ask questions that lead to enlightening answers than from any inherent moral or ethical insolvability. The problem is, many people are unsure how to start analyzing an ethical conflict, what questions to ask, and how to proceed.

Our teaching of applied ethics during the past decade has led to our development of the RESOLVEDD strategy of ethical decision making. It provides a clearly applicable and easily remembered approach to the complexities of ethical conflicts encountered in everyday life. It does not simplify such conflicts, but helps to guide one through a process of arriving at a well-reasoned decision.

The first half of the book presents an applicable overview of ethics, some basic, useful ethical values, the RESOLVEDD strategy of analysis, and provides three sample analyses using the strategy. The second half presents forty-two personal ethical conflicts that might be encountered by employees in various occupations. The purpose of these cases is to challenge the student to apply the RESOLVEDD strategy to develop the best decision possible in each case. The effort to do so offers the student opportunities to examine the case from varying perspectives, sharpen his or her grasp of important ethical principles, and to assert, analyze, and defend value judgments based on them.

The personal ethical conflicts presented in the book are rarely clear-cut. There are usually a number of compelling options for resolving each conflict. Moreover, these conflicts do not simply present the question of whether or not to act ethically. There are usually significant ethical advantages and disadvantages to several of the main options relevant to each conflict. To decide in such contexts, the reader must make and defend value judgments regarding which ethical principles are relevant and most important for the case.

The personal ethical conflicts presented here are typical of the work-a-day lives of lower-level managers and their employees. We have largely avoided the kinds of ethical issues confronted by top-level managers and directors of organizations. Current textbooks in ethics present many such cases. But they less frequently present students with the kinds of ethical problems confronted by workers at lower organizational levels.

These issues confronting lower-level employees are important for at least four reasons. First, most people begin their careers at the bottom of organizational ladders. If they have studied only the broad ethical issues confronted by those at the top, they may be ill equipped to address the issues of day-to-day work they confront early in their careers. Second, the approach a manager takes to ethical issues confronted later in life results in part from habits of thought developed earlier. Many of the same ethical principles and values are relevant to ethical issues on all levels of an organization. Students can develop a clear understanding of these principles and their applications and exceptions by studying issues relevant to employees at lower organizational levels. Third, top-level executives should be well informed about the viewpoints of their subordinates. One of the best ways for them to understand these views is to confront and analyze the kinds of personal ethical conflicts addressed by lower-level employees often contain challenging and enlightening issues that are well worth analysis in their own right.

The personal ethical conflicts presented here are our own creations. Most are adapted from newspaper reports, journal articles, and personal experiences of friends and acquaintances. The characters are fictional, as are the companies, institutions, and the particular personal relationships described. However, the background information presented in each case is, to the best of our knowledge, accurate. The cases present fictional characters facing problems that may arise in real working environments.

The RESOLVEDD strategy integrates a model of decision making with certain ways of thinking essential to the study of ethics. The strategy directs the student or manager to make a decision after having analyzed and evaluated both main sources of ethical justification: consequences and principles. It helps the student survey the possible solutions to a given conflict, identify the significant consequences of each main solution, and state the ethical principles upheld and violated by each one before proceeding to evaluate them and make a decision.

The RESOLVEDD strategy is based more on a certain practical and common-sense approach to ethics than on a philosophical theory. Our approach does not result from an attempt to apply any of the great theories of ethics such as utilitarianism, natural law, or Kantian or Aristotelian ethics. These theories are the result of philosophers' attempts to clarify and systematize certain basic intuitions believed to be fundamental to the moral point of view. That point of view can, however, be described in other ways, independent of these theories. The approach we take is certainly not inconsistent with these theories, but neither is it based on an exclusive commitment to any one of them.

This book can be used as a general supplement to most of the more comprehensive ethics texts that are currently popular in college courses in ethics. Because it is neutral regarding the main theories of ethics, it is compatible with most such texts. Its day-to-day orientation adds a practical dimension to the more theoretical level of discussion in many of those texts.

ACKNOWLEDGMENTS

This book is born of the growing awareness among teachers of applied ethics that ethical decision making involves ways of thinking that differ in significant respects from those appropriate to the philosophical study of ethics. Our understanding of these differences has developed gradually over the years in the many classes we have taught in ethics, business ethics, and medical ethics. This book brings to fruition many ideas and lessons growing out of a long process of reflection, dialogue, and experimentation, spurred on by the commitment to improve the value of our teaching for our students.

Raymond Pfeiffer first became aware of the need for a decision-making strategy when teaching bioethics to Delta College nursing students in 1979. He found that ethical theories traditionally studied in courses in philosophical ethics have limited value for making decisions in everyday contexts. Professor Richard A. Wright, a consultant sponsored by the National Endowment for the Humanities, suggested the importance of offering a practical strategy for students to apply when confronting ethical issues on the job. Pfeiffer's attempts to use Wright's own Situation Assessment Procedure led him to develop an early version of the decision-making strategy presented here. He initially used the word DIAGNOSE as an acronym to help students master the steps of the strategy. Although the strategy worked well, Pfeiffer was not fully satisfied with the acronym. A colleague, Max Thomas, suggested in 1987 that the word SOLVE might be adapted as a better acronym. This word had other shortcomings, which were later addressed in developing the acronym RESOLVEDD as it is presented here.

Ralph Forsberg's teaching of applied ethics at Harper College in Palatine, Illinois, and at Loyola University of Chicago had led him to become aware that many cases presented by texts in business ethics had limitations. Typically, the cases required the student to assume the role of a top executive. He undertook, beginning in the early 1980s, to develop cases that would be more typical of the kinds of employment his students would have during college and in the first few years beyond. He received important encouragement in this endeavor from professors Patricia A. Werhane and David T. Ozar at Loyola.

When we (the authors) became colleagues at Delta College in 1989, we discovered the complementary nature of our interests. If there is any one moral theorist to which we owe a special debt, it is Bernard Gert. We have found a version of his notion of the moral rules to be helpful in applying the RESOLVEDD strategy. We have not, however, adopted all his moral rules or the precise formulations of those rules that emerge from his careful and insightful analysis.

Our students in medical ethics and business ethics classes over the past decade have helped us sharpen and season our approach. Mary Sue Anderson, Michelle Cobb, Cassandra Collier, Steven W. May, Raquel L. Mondol, Cynthia L. Ott, and James A. Wood have graciously allowed us to adapt their ideas and writings for this work.

The free and open environment at Delta College has contributed immeasurably to the development of this book. Delta administrators such as Deans Owen Homeister, Brenda Beckman, and Betty Jones have continually encouraged innovation and, at times, offered much needed support. Our colleague in philosophy, Professor Linda Plackowski, was of special help, daring to struggle with some of our early ideas. Many of our colleagues in the divisions of Nursing, Business, Technology, and Allied Health have reviewed our ideas and encouraged us to try them out on their students. In particular, professors Jessie Dolson, Louise Goodburne, Bruce Leppien, Ion Keefer, and John Flattery have provided time, energy, thoughts, and opportunities to work with their students, and deserve our special gratitude.

The philosophy editor at Wadsworth, Ken King, has been an important source of encouragement and guidance. The professors who reveiwed the manuscript for Wadsworth made many insightful suggestions that helped us to improve the final product significantly. Our thanks to: Cyril Dwiggins, Dickinson College; Ida M. Jones, California State University—Fresno; John L. Longeway, University of Wisconsin—Parkside; Michael S. Pritchard, Western Michigan University;

George L. Stengren, Central Michigan University; Art Wolfe, Michigan State University.

Like other textbook authors, we owe a debt to the many thinkers from whom we have shamelessly borrowed and adapted many ideas and approaches. Our work has grown from participation in an extended community of teachers, scholars, and philosophers whose integrity and wisdom have inspired and motivated us.

CHAPTER I

❏ ❏ ❏ ❏ ❏ ❏ ❏

Ethics and Ethical Decision Making

❏ 1.1 A Personal Ethical Conflict: The Case of the Hidden Cameras

You are working for the summer on the maintenance crew of a local school district. During your first week's work at Reidell High School, you learn that it is well known that computers and VCRs have been stolen regularly from Reidell during the school year. The culprits have apparently eluded detection despite the efforts of administrators.

When you report for work at the beginning of your second week, your boss, the head of maintenance, takes you aside for a confidential talk. She explains that the superintendent of schools has authorized the installation of hidden video cameras at the loading dock and in employee lounges and computer labs at Reidell. The cameras will apparently be monitored by security personnel. She explains that you must not mention these facts to anyone, and then tells you to install them. You feel uneasy about the order but initially agree to do so.

Having just completed a course in ethics, you are concerned about violations of privacy that may result from the hidden cameras. You worry about the matter all day, and then decide to take action. You decide this is a serious matter appropriately addressed by those at the top. You boldly make an appointment with the superintendent and meet him within the week. At the meeting, you state your concerns, and listen to his responses. He explains that the surveillance will be confidential, the information gathered will be carefully protected, and no laws will be violated. You offer ethical objections to his views, but

1

to no avail. You leave convinced more than ever that the surveillance is ethically wrong on a number of grounds. Believing what you do and having done what you did, how should you now proceed, and why?

Such a situation would present you with a personal ethical conflict. Whatever you do, you must choose. Whether you recognize it or not, ethical values are at stake. If you do nothing, you are allowing a wrong to occur that you might have prevented. If you take your objection to the local newspaper or the board of education, the surveillance may become public knowledge and thus ineffective. You may be stepping beyond your bounds as a temporary maintenance employee, or end up damaging your own reputation. Due to the complexities and the values at stake, such a situation may present you with an agonizing choice.

This book offers a strategy that will help you respond to such personal ethical conflicts. A perfect solution to such a conflict would be one in which you violate no ethical values and yet achieve your most important goals. However, when perfect solutions are unavailable, you must settle for the best alternative. The decision-making strategy developed in this book shows you how to address a number of questions that can help you find the best solution.

To make a responsible decision, you should consider the choices available, the outcomes of each, and their likely impacts on people's lives. Just which ethical values are upheld and which are violated by the alternatives are essential questions. Which of these values are important for your decision and which are unimportant must be carefully weighed. Whether your ethical values are more important than some of your personal goals may present a further challenge.

We assume that ethical values are important to everyone, and that everyone wants to make decisions that compromise these values as little as reasonably possible. The process of evaluating and choosing among ethical values, personal goals and the likely consequences of actions is far from simple. However, this process is clarified and facilitated by use of the RESOLVEDD strategy of decision making presented in Chapter 3.

The purpose of the RESOLVEDD strategy is to help you arrive at decisions that implement an ethical point of view. Consideration of certain basic aspects of such a point of view may help you understand the spirit of the strategy. The purpose of pursuing the RESOLVEDD strategy is, in short, to arrive at a decision by which you achieve your most important goals while compromising ethical values as little as reasonably and ethically justifiable.

❏ 1.2 Ethics, Judgments, Principles, and Values

Ethics may be viewed as the study of the justification of ethical value judgments. An ethical value judgment is a judgment of right or wrong, good or bad, better or worse, virtue or vice, or what ought or ought not to be done. Justification involves giving reasons or evidence for the truth or falsehood of a given judgment.

Consider the following value judgment as it applies to the case of the hidden cameras:

Value 1. It is wrong to report the installation of the hidden cameras to the local newspaper.

To determine the likely truth or falsehood of such a judgment, you examine the evidence for and against it. To cite and evaluate such evidence is to proceed within the discipline of ethics.

Ethical principles are commonly used to justify ethical judgments. To justify Value 1, you might state,

Principle 1. A person should not report private matters to the newspapers.

This is an ethical principle. It makes an ethical value judgment about a range of cases, not simply one particular situation. Ethical principles are important because we use them as reasons to think that a given decision is a good one or not so good.

People often refer to their ethical principles as "ethical values." If you say, "telling the newspapers violates my ethical values" you may mean simply that telling the newspapers violates some of your ethical principles. The terms "ethical values" and "ethical principles" are used almost interchangeably throughout this text.

People at times disagree about ethical values. Such disagreement may result from a number of differences. There may, for example, be disagreement over the proper formulation of ethical principles. Thus, you might disagree with Principle 1 on the grounds that some private matters are best reported to the newspaper. However, people some-times disagree over whether or not and how an ethical principle applies to a specific situation. You might argue that although Principle 1 is true, it does not apply to the case of the hidden cameras because that case does not concern a private matter. People also may disagree over the question of which ethical principles are most important in a given situation. You might argue that Principle 1 is not nearly as important as the principle that people have a duty to act to prevent others from violating people's rights.

☐ 1.3 An Ethical Point of View: The Principle of Equal Consideration of Interests

This book assumes that you want to improve your ability to make ethical value judgments. It assumes that you want to approach personal ethical conflicts from an ethical point of view. Such a point of view is expressed by the principle of equal consideration of interests (ECI), which may be summarized as follows:

> The principle of equal consideration of interests (ECI): You should make judgments, decisions and act in ways which treat the interests and well-being of others as no less important than your own.*

ECI does not imply that ethical behavior means treating the interests and well-being of others as more important than your own. Rather, it implies fairness and impartiality in your dealings with other people. It requires, for example, that you not report the hidden cameras to the newspaper simply because of your dislike of the superintendent. It requires that your own personal likes and dislikes not count as reasons to think something is right or wrong, or ought or ought not to be done.

ECI requires that you use your ethical principles as reasons, and that you apply these principles equally to yourself and to others. If you believe it is wrong to install hidden cameras in Reidell High, then you should object to installing them in other schools with similar problems of theft. Whether you are the superintendent or a maintenance person is irrelevant to the ethical reasons why the cameras should not be installed. The ethical person applies ethical principles impartially, recognizing the equal moral value of the lives and well-being of all people.

An ethical decision, then, is a decision that (1) implements an ethical point of view, not violating ECI; (2) compromises ethical principles as little as reasonably and ethically justifiable; and (3) lets you achieve

* Peter Singer, *Practical Ethics* (Cambridge, England: Cambridge University Press, 1979), p. 19.

your personal goals to as great an extent as consistent with points 1 and 2.

☐ 1.4 Conflicting Goals

Our personal goals sometimes conflict with our ethical value judgments. In deciding what to do about the hidden cameras, you might decide that on ethical grounds you should oppose them, but that doing so might cost you your job. Furthermore, the job may in fact be important to you. This sort of personal conflict must be taken seriously, and may be addressed by several strategies.

First, you should investigate the nature of the threat to your personal goals. How real is that threat? Are you protected by a union contract? Do school district policies provide protection for employees who complain? Are there policies that provide due process for employees before being fired? Could you get support from your supervisor or some other person in a position of authority? Further investigation might reveal that the risk to your job is minimal.

Second, you should consider the importance of your personal goals in the case. Are other summer jobs available? How long would it take to obtain one? How much money might you lose, and how important, all things considered, is that loss?

Third, you should investigate the weight and firmness of your ethical beliefs in the situation. Are the hidden cameras a serious invasion of privacy? How serious? What is worth sacrificing in order to oppose it?

Fourth, you should calculate the chances of success in proceeding to act on your ethical convictions. Are you likely to obtain the support of others in a fight against the hidden cameras? Who might support you, why, and how might you obtain such support?

Fifth, you will likely benefit by discussing the issues with other people. Such discussions may reveal unnoticed options, new information, different perspectives, and alternate value judgments and may expand your understanding and grasp of the issues. As a result, you may be more likely to arrive at a decision in which you can have confidence.

A responsible decision should not ignore your own legitimate or ethically defensible personal goals. To the extent that our goals in life are legitimate, we owe it to ourselves to take them seriously. Ethics do not require us to ignore self-interest or make personal sacrifices for trivial or ill-considered reasons.

The goal of the RESOLVEDD strategy of ethical decision making, introduced in Chapter 3, is to help you arrive at decisions with which you can live—in the full sense. An ethical decision is one in which you can take pride and willingly explain to others. Ethical decision making can help you maintain your integrity and live with a clear conscience.

❑ 1.5 Ethical Justification

Decision making in a situation of personal ethical conflict should be based on assessment of the evidence for and against the various options. Study of this evidence reveals which option is most clearly justified. Justification thus refers to the evidence for and against a given judgment. Ethical decision making requires that you judge the significance of the evidence to arrive at the most clearly justified choice given the circumstances.

Two main kinds of reasons can be offered as evidence to justify an ethical decision. You can offer reasons based on the effects of the decision and reasons based on relevant ethical principles. A responsible decision regarding a personal ethical conflict should result from careful evaluation of both kinds of reasons both for and against all the available options.

In the case of the hidden cameras, you might argue that your duty to uphold the right to privacy of your fellow employees requires you to carry your objections beyond the superintendent. In that case, your duty to uphold the right to privacy is cited as an important moral principle that you should uphold. Because this principle is relevant to the case, it may be offered as a reason to think it is justifiable to complain to the school board.

Another reason to complain might be that the failure to do so may lead to certain important consequences. If the cameras are installed and monitored as planned, lots of information will be gathered about employees. Much of this will be of a personal and even private nature. The cameras may well detect some employee comments that cast the employee in rather unfavorable light. This in turn may lead to the firing of some employees for unjust reasons.

In making any decision, it is important to identify and evaluate both the relevant ethical principles and consequences. In the RESOLVEDD strategy, the consequences are identified in Steps 4 and 5, and the principles in Step 6. There is no simple procedure for evaluating the relevant reasons for and against a given option. However, some reasons are better than others, and this difference can be discerned by comparing and contrasting the options and the principles and consequences that support them. The task of doing this is Step 7 in the RESOLVEDD strategy, explained in Chapters 3 and 4 and illustrated in Chapter 5.

☐ 1.6 Ethical Values: Justifiable Exceptions

Ethical values are principles that help us make decisions implementing the ethical point of view. Ethicists largely agree that any principle must have the following three characteristics to be an ethical principle for a given person. First, the principle must be important to the person; second, the person must believe that all people should treat it as important; and third, the person must believe that it should be applied in accordance with the principle of equal consideration of interests.

1. For a given principle to be someone's ethical principle, it should be important to that person. That is, it should be important enough to override some of that person's personal preferences. If honesty is one of your ethical principles, then you are willing to avoid deceiving others even if it causes you personal inconvenience. A person who is willing to lie for a petty gain is one for whom honesty is probably not a real ethical value.

2. For a given principle to be someone's ethical principle, the person should believe that other people should also live in accordance with it. This requirement rules out many uniquely personal preferences. Thus, your preference for plum-flavored ice cream is probably not an ethical principle for you. As much as you may prize that flavor of ice cream, your preference is not one of your ethical values or principles unless you believe earnestly that all people have an obligation to prefer it, too.

People ordinarily believe that their ethical principles are principles that others should follow. Those who prize honesty typically believe that other people should prize it, too. They act in accordance with their own ethical principles in the firm belief that the world would generally be a better place if all people acted in accordance with those principles.

3. For a principle to be an ethical principle for a given person, that

person must believe that it should be followed by oneself (and others) in a way that implements the principle of ECI. If honesty is one of your ethical principles, then you will not be honest merely when convenient. Doing so would be to treat the interests of others as less important than your own.

These three requirements do not imply that an ethical principle should never be violated. There may be situations in which it is impossible to act in ways that do not violate any ethical principles. You might find yourself in a situation in which every option violates either the principle of truth (you should not deceive people) or the principle of harm (you should not do things that harm people). If so, you must choose between the options and thus violate one of these principles. To act ethically, you will try to choose which option violates which principle more seriously, and which option upholds which principle more seriously. Such choices are discussed more in Chapters 3 and 4, and illustrated in Chapter 5.

Although ethical principles are important, you need not assume that they are absolute or universally inviolable. It is possible, although controversial, to recognize the importance of certain ethical principles and to implement an ethical point of view without maintaining that any principles make absolute, unexceptionable, or inviolable demands on your life. An ethical principle may be important even if you recognize certain ethically justifiable exceptions to it. To recognize the existence of such exceptions is not necessarily to reduce the importance of that ethical principle. If you recognize exceptions (such as capital punishment or passive euthanasia) to the principle that one should not kill people, you may still object just as strongly to the murder of an innocent, blameless individual. Whether or not you recognize capital punishment or passive euthanasia as ethically justifiable may be irrelevant to the question of how wrong it is to murder an innocent person.

Whether ethical principles are absolute or not is in one sense irrelevant to ethical decision making. To act ethically, you must have ethical principles, recognize their importance, avoid surrendering them without strong ethical justification, and apply them consistently, equally, and fairly in all your relations to others. Whether those principles are peculiar to yourself, or widely held in society or the world, or whether you believe they make absolute, unexceptionable demands on you, need not be answered in order to make responsible ethical decisions in specific cases.

☐ 1.7 Why Should I Act Ethically?

One of the great questions of philosophical ethics is, "Why should I act ethically?" It has been addressed by many of the great philosophers, beginning with Socrates, Plato, and Aristotle. A full answer is outside the scope of this book. However, it is worth noting briefly one direction such an answer might take.

To act ethically is, at the very least, to strive to act in ways that do not hurt other people; that respect their dignity, individuality, and uniquely moral value; and that treat others as equally important as oneself. If you believe these are worthwhile goals, then you have reason to strive to act ethically. If you do not believe these are worthwhile goals for human beings to pursue, then you may believe it is not important to act ethically.

People who renounce the importance of ethics either renounce these goals completely, or they believe that such goals can just as well be pursued on occasion, when convenient, to maintain appearances, and can just as well be ignored when inconvenient. Probably very few people renounce such goals altogether. A lifestyle characterized by complete lack of ethical behavior would be so antisocial that it might well result in imprisonment or social ostracism.

Many people, however, seem to think that they can live their lives in ways that are ethical much of the time, but unethical at other times. Such an intermittently unethical lifestyle has many pitfalls, some of which are worth listing briefly here.

1. Such a lifestyle, when discovered by others, usually leads them to lose trust in the person.

2. Those who discover such behavior sometimes seek to retaliate against the offenders.

3. Living in such ways sometimes leads people to act unethically at the wrong time. We all rely on our habits and inclinations when there is too little time to deliberate. Unethical behavior weakens our inclinations to act ethically, and may lead us, in times of stress, to act in ways we later regret.

4. Living in such ways may make us feel guilty if we have been brought up in families and societies that established in us a sense of conscience.

5. Acting ethically only at selected times leads us to lose trust in ourselves. As a result, we may become worried, unsure, and anxious about

the possibility that we may make a mistake and act unethically at the wrong times.

6. Acting unethically, when we choose, leads us to occasional violations of many values that are important to us, such as those presented in the next chapter. It leads us to violate honesty, loyalty, consistency, fairness, and many other important ethical principles.

7. The intermittently unethical lifestyle may violate our religious beliefs.

In summary, the intermittently unethical lifestyle may lead to a life of more misery than the ethical lifestyle. Of course, this does not prove conclusively that each of us will live better if we strive to act ethically all the time. Whether that is true is a matter each person must judge as life progresses. However, in making such choices, we should not ignore the lessons provided by the cultural, religious, literary, and moral traditions in which we live. Our values have emerged from those traditions, and are deeply enmeshed in them. They may shed important light on the hard decisions we face in life.

CHAPTER 2

❑　❑　❑　❑　❑　❑　❑

Ethical Principles

❑ 2.1 The Importance of Ethical Principles

Ethical principles are important for ethical decision making for two main reasons. First, they express our most deeply held convictions. As such, we are said to be obligated to uphold our ethical principles. That is, if we want to act ethically and a given principle expresses one of our ethical convictions, then we have an ethical obligation to uphold that principle.

Second, ethical principles play an important role in the effort to arrive at a decision about what is best in a given case. Because of their moral force, we seek solutions that uphold them. Applying these principles to a given case helps us determine what our ethical convictions demand of us.

When our ethical principles conflict with one another in a given case, we must determine which possible solution sacrifices ethical value the least. Although this is sometimes difficult, we can often find good reason to think that one solution sacrifices ethical value less than does another.

A number of ethical principles are shared widely among members of our society and those beyond. The following list may be helpful when you try to make decisions in the presence of personal ethical conflicts. The list is not a definitive or complete ethical system. Certainly other ethical principles are important, but are not listed here. And you may find other formulations of these principles to be more familiar or helpful in making ethical decisions. These formulations are offered merely as coherent statements of some widely and deeply held intuitions about ethical value.

You need not assume that the following ethical principles are absolutes. If they express important ethical values of yours, and you are committed to trying to live by the ethical point of view, then you will find strong reason to try not to violate them. The ethical point of view need not require that you never violate such principles. It demands that you do so only to uphold some other ethical principle that is more justifiably upheld in the circumstances. Ethically, you must not violate them solely for purposes of self-interest.

☐ 2.2. Some Moral Rules

Broadly held ethical principles are sometimes referred to as "moral rules." Such principles may help you apply the principle of equal consideration of interests to specific contexts. The following moral rules can be particularly useful in making decisions in the workplace.

The Principle of Honesty

In its most basic form, the principle of honesty is the principle that you should not deceive other people. There are, of course, many ways of deceiving people, and all of them contradict this principle. One form of deception is lying, which may be described as stating what you believe is false in order to mislead someone intentionally. Another is stating a half-truth, deliberately omitting information in order to mislead. Another is the failure to speak up at all, when you know the truth and know that silence will result in someone having false beliefs. In addition, there are many ways of misleading people while stating the truth. The principle of honesty can also be violated in various nonverbal ways, such as conveying a false impression through misleading body language.

It is important to note that withholding information does not always violate the principle of honesty. You can withhold information from another person, even one who has a right to it, without deceiving that person. You might frankly and openly refuse to tell the person what you know.

The principle of honesty is important because it is the source of trust, which is essential for social relationships of all kinds. It is also important because people normally expect to be treated honestly. Moreover, people usually lead others to believe that they will treat them honestly and nondeceptively.

The Principle of Harm

The principle of harm requires that you avoid doing things that harm other people or damage their projects, efforts, or property. We have a strong duty to avoid making the lives of others worse. This duty is essential for social harmony. Furthermore, unless we respect the well-being of others, we cannot expect them to respect ours.

The principle of harm does not require us to improve the lot of others. It merely requires us to avoid harming others in direct and indirect ways. It is an idea embodied in the U.S. Constitution and in the laws of most countries. The principle of harm is essential to the idea of legal rights, and is an important basis for each of the other ethical principles described here.

The Principle of Fidelity

The principle of fidelity may be summarized as the principle that you should fulfill your commitments and act faithfully. You should, first, fulfill the agreements, pledges, and promises you make. Second, you should fulfill the special obligations of the relationships you maintain.

We make commitments in a variety of ways. Sometimes we sign our names in writing, and sometimes we verbally commit ourselves to do certain things. We make commitments by entering certain relationships, and also by continuing to participate in them. When others have expectations of us, we know what they are, and we allow these expectations to continue, then we are responsible to fulfill them.

Fidelity is an essential value for all human relationships and institutions, and it lies at the core of trust and cooperation. It is the tie that binds, carrying us beyond an isolated individualism, and motivating us to implement the principles of honesty and harm. It is intensely personal in nature, and violations of the principle of fidelity are often resented profoundly by others.

The requirements of the principle of fidelity differ widely in different contexts. Within our families, fidelity leads us to respect privacy and provide emotional support. Sometimes referred to as *loyalty*, fidelity may require trustworthiness and the willingness to put the well-being of others before our own. At work, fidelity requires that we follow the standard procedures of the workplace, respecting lines of authority and established decision-making procedures. Fidelity to our subordinates, co-workers, associates, and superiors requires that when we have a problem with their performance, we first tell them the problem, offering them a chance to solve it before we take it to their superiors. It requires, moreover, that we treat our subordinates fairly and equally. Beyond this, fidelity implies that we fulfill the duties of our jobs, maintain certain levels of performance, act to support and assist, and provide timely notice when we plan to terminate employment.

There are, of course, limits to the demands of fidelity. Fidelity is not the highest ethical value, and usually does not justify actions that violate the principle of equal consideration of interests, or are unethical or illegal. To promote your employer's best interest is not viewed, for example, by legal authorities as justifying your violation of the law. Concealing pertinent product information from a customer may help make a sale while it violates the customer's right to know, or even harms the customer. Such concealment is generally viewed as unethical conduct that exceeds the demands of fidelity to one's employer.

To follow the principle of fidelity is to act in ways that implement the principle of harm toward those with whom we have special relationships. But fidelity requires us to do more than simply avoid harming others. Fidelity encourages us to contribute to the lot of others in various ways appropriate to the relationships we have.

The Principle of Autonomy

Autonomy is the ability to act in informed, considered, rational ways that are largely free from coercion. The autonomous person is responsible for one's deeds, and may be said to deserve praise or blame for them. Having access to information that is available and essential to making a good decision, such a person decides on his or her own what is best in the circumstances. The principle of autonomy is the principle that we have a duty to allow and enable other people to act in informed, considered, rational ways.

There are many ways of violating the principle of autonomy. One may exaggerate, deceive people, omit relevant information, or use threats and other forms of coercion. Most people who violate this principle do so from the desire to ensure that others act as they want.

But one can also violate the principle of autonomy by simply acting carelessly, without any particular motive.

This is a principle we take seriously in our society. We spend more money and energy promoting this principle than perhaps any other. Our entire educational system is directed to help other people develop their autonomy. Laws that forbid deception in business, government, and other areas of life are designed to respect and facilitate autonomous actions.

The principle of autonomy is intimately and reciprocally related to other important moral principles. It is part of the basis or justification of the principle of honesty. One major reason to treat others honestly is that doing so helps them act autonomously. Furthermore, the principle of honesty offers reason to value the principle of autonomy. If you value the principle of honesty, then you value a principle that upholds people's autonomy. The principle of honesty is a part of the principle of autonomy.

The principle of autonomy is part of the justification of the principles of harm and honesty. One important reason not to harm others or deceive them is that doing so violates the principle of autonomy. These three principles are closely intertwined.

Fidelity also requires respect of the principle of autonomy, and vice versa. An important part of most human relationships is the need for each party to respect the autonomy of the other. In most cases, one cannot respect the principle of autonomy without acting in accord with the principle of fidelity, and vice versa.

The principle of harm is also fundamentally and reciprocally connected to the principle of autonomy. Violations of autonomy often harm people, either directly or indirectly. When needed information is withheld from people, they may react with resentment or anger when they discover the reality. To violate people's autonomy may thwart their goals, leading them to suffer the consequences. To violate the principle of harm may also involve violation of the principle of autonomy, as we may harm people by ignoring their right to know something.

The Principle of Confidentiality

Closely connected to the principles already presented is the principle of confidentiality. Although it is, in a sense, derived from a certain combination of them, it is worth considering separately because of its special relevance to the workplace. Indeed, confidentiality may be viewed as a uniquely professional work-related or role-based ethical principle.

This is the principle that some information should not be released to people outside of certain circles. These circles or groups may be defined by the roles of the people within them, by their duties, responsibilities, and need to have access to certain information in order to perform their jobs appropriately. Respecting the principle of confidentiality protects certain people from being harmed by information falling into the wrong hands. It may prevent violations of the right to privacy.

Whether or not information is properly confidential in nature may be discerned by considering three factors: (1) the potential effects of releasing the information; (2) the origin of the information; and (3) the intent of those who might be affected by releasing it. If the release of certain information to someone could harm a third party in some significant way, the information is probably best treated as confidential, and maintained within the appropriate circles. Consideration of the origin of information can also indicate its confidential nature. Information obtained from medical records, corporate research plans, or private conversations that have been overheard is probably best treated as confidential. If someone has a right that certain information be kept confidential, and would likely intend that it be kept confidential, there is reason to treat it accordingly. Consideration of any one of these three factors may provide sufficient evidence that information falls under the principle of confidentiality. The principles of harm, honesty, autonomy, and fidelity may offer justification for treating information as confidential.

The Principle of Lawfulness

It is important to recognize that there are four main sources of law. First and most basic are *constitutional* laws, which define the political procedures of the nation, its states, and their subdivisions. Second are *legislative* laws, which are passed by formal votes of the federal and state legislatures, and signed into law by the executive branches of governments. Third are *executive* or *administrative* laws, which are interpretations of the first two by the executive branch, which is charged with implementing constitutional and legislative laws. Fourth are laws formed by *judicial decisions,* which interpret and apply to specific cases the constitutional, legislative, and executive laws. The principle of lawfulness is the duty to follow these laws, to cooperate with those who act lawfully in implementing and enforcing them, and to seek to change them only by lawful and ethical means.

Although it is certainly true that not all laws are just or ethically justifiable, there is still a general, ethically based duty to obey the law, especially in a largely free and broadly democratic society. In such a society, all citizens have potential influence in making the laws. If they do not find the time to exercise that influence, or choose not to do so, their continued presence in that society may be interpreted as a general agreement to abide by all of its laws. The principle of fidelity may thus be one basis for the obligation to act accordingly.

Many laws are justified by their success in fulfilling the principles of harm and autonomy. Violations of the law may harm others directly or indirectly, or violate their autonomy, and are accordingly unjustifiable. Such considerations may offer a powerful justification for following many laws, even if not all of them.

If a person tries to change a law but is unsuccessful because he or she is in a political minority, that person has the option of leaving the geographical area that is under the jurisdiction of that law. If the person chooses to stay, he or she may continue to oppose the law while at the same time being bound by the principle of lawfulness to follow the law. In so doing, the person is a part of what is known as the *loyal opposition*. The person is loyal in not violating the law at the same time he or she works to oppose it.

If a law is unjust and someone opposes it unsuccessfully, that person may resort to *civil disobedience*. This includes public violation of the law, to dramatize the need for change. Whether or not civil disobedience is ethically justifiable is an old and complicated issue, which need not be addressed here. It should be noted, however, that civil disobedience does not include private violation of the law for the sake of one's own advantage. The citizen who quietly cheats in paying income tax because the tax seems too large is not engaged in civil disobedience. Such a violation of the law violates the principle of lawfulness.

Laws are often made to protect the rights of individuals. Violations of the law may thus also involve violations of individual moral or political rights. In the next section, we consider the nature and importance of rights in general, and a few specific rights.

❑ 2.3 Rights and Duties

A right is a justified claim to something. That is, if someone has a right to something, then there is good reason for that person to have that thing. If you have a legal right, then the legal system declares that you may have good reason to exercise that right. Laws are often statements of legal rights.

Rights are options that you may or may not choose to exercise. Even if you do not in fact exercise a right, you may still be said to have it. However, a right is not in fact recognized, respected, or realized unless the opportunity to exercise it is a viable option that you can enact without some penalty from a source that is external to you. If you have a right to vote, but are penalized for doing so by your employer, then your right to vote has not been respected by the employer. But failing to vote in order not to miss your favorite TV program is no limitation on your right. Missing the program may be a loss, but is not a penalty imposed on you by an external source. Of course, some cases can't be definitely classified. But they can be judged by the endeavor, however difficult, to locate them on the spectrum between limitations that are externally imposed, on the one hand, and your own desires, on the other.

If you have an ethical right to something, then you may choose to exercise it without acting unethically. If you have a right to something, then someone else has a duty either to fulfill the right or at the least not to interfere with your effort to fulfill it. If you have a right to a tax refund, then the government has a duty to provide it. If you have a right to freedom of speech, then the government and its citizens have, at least, a duty not to interfere.

Ethical rights differ from legal rights in several ways. The former may or may not be upheld by the law. A legal right, however, is a right that is guaranteed by the law. Only ethical reasons and principles can justify the belief that you have a given ethical right. The mere presence of a legal right, however, is not by itself any proof that this right is ethically justified. It may exist as a result of certain political maneuvering that lacks ethical justification. However, ethical reasons and principles can sometimes give good reason to think that there ought to be a legal right. Most good laws are partially justified by some ethical reasons or principles.

Ethical rights may be justified in part by other ethical principles. The principles of harm and autonomy offer good reasons to think that government has an ethical right to require corporations to avoid false advertising. If false advertising were allowed, more people would be misled, their autonomy curtailed, and their money wasted.

Moral and ethical rights are interrelated with moral rules. You may be said to have a right to be treated by others in accordance with the moral rules just described. The justifications of those rules offer good reason to think that people ought to be treated accordingly and that failing to do so is ordinarily wrong. Moreover, various ethical rights may offer good reasons to think that people should uphold certain moral rules.

People sometimes make very forceful and insistent statements that certain people have certain ethical rights. Such statements may sound convincing, and even intimidating. But you should not therefore assume that they are justifiable. Such people may be upset about some matter and overstate their case. It is important not to be persuaded by the authoritative sound of the language of rights.

One effective way to approach a statement that there is a certain right is to ask what duties are involved, who has them, and why. Answers to such questions may well lead you to discover that such a statement is unjustified. Although it may at first sound plausible that someone has a certain right, consideration of the nature and justification of the corresponding duty may reveal cause for doubt. Most rights imply limitations on the actions of others; some justify burdens on others.

Consider the manager who asserts that she has a right to fire a subordinate. If she means that she has a legal right to do so, consideration of the law and policies of the company should resolve the question. If she means she has an ethical right to do so, consideration of the corresponding duties may help you evaluate the implications and justification of her claim.

If the manager has an ethical right to fire the employee, then her superiors have an ethical duty to allow her to do so. If, however, the employee is productive, reliable, respected by his peers, and cooperates with other managers, the manager may have no reason to fire him beyond the presence of a personality conflict. Indeed, firing him might be unfair to him and do more harm than good for the company. In such a case, upper management might well have no duty to allow him to be fired, and might better transfer him to another division of the company in order to resolve the problem. Thus, considering the duty associated with a supposed right may suggest factors that can help determine the existence of the right. Identifying the duty may help you clarify and evaluate the justification of the supposed right.

❑ 2.4 Some Important Ethical Rights

The number of nameable rights is very large. Some, however, are particularly useful in evaluating ethical conflicts at the workplace. The following rights and their corresponding duties express important ethical values, but need not be thought of as absolutely inviolable. Like other ethical principles, you may view them as offering strong but not absolute ethical reason to act in certain ways.

The Right to Know

The right to know is closely connected to the duty to inform. People in certain roles and occupations have a right to know certain kinds of information. And those in certain relationships to those others sometimes have ethical duties and sometimes legal duties to provide them with the information.

If an auto mechanic discovers that the brakes in your car are worn down, the mechanic has a duty to inform you, who have a right to that information. However, although you may have a right to know something, there may be circumstances where another person may not have a duty to inform. Rights are options, and you may have a right to know without choosing to exercise the right, without trying to find out. Although you have a right to know that there are better cars on the market than the one you are now driving, the mechanic does not necessarily have a duty to tell you (unless, of course, your present car is unsafe).

It is important to recognize that one can violate the duty to give information without violating the principle of honesty. Consider the mechanic who is having a busy day, frustrated by many interruptions. She might neglect to note on the work order that the wheel bearings are low on grease. Although she violated the duty to give information, she did not intentionally conceal it.

The Right to Privacy

The right to privacy is the right to control information about yourself, or access to it. To have this right is not necessarily to exercise it. You reveal information about yourself whenever you appear in public, or engage in cooperative work. It is common knowledge that in certain situations, some information about people will normally be made available to other people. Although much of this information is not clearly of a private nature, some of it may be. You may give information of a personal nature to your colleagues without clarifying its personal or private nature.

Giving personal information to others does not automatically count as permission to pass it on. An evaluation of employee work performance is private information and should not be passed on by the employer without the employee's permission. The misuse of information about a person may itself violate the right to privacy.

It is possible for someone to violate your right to privacy even if you give permission to obtain the information. If you give permission under threat or coercion, the person who gathers the information may be violating your right to privacy. Such permission should be given of your own free will.

Someone who has the right to know does not necessarily have the right to use any means available to obtain the information. Your employer may have the right to know who is stealing supplies from the stock room but not have the right to invade your privacy in order to catch the thief. The right to know is not identical to the right to obtain information.

Your right to privacy can be violated at home or at work. Beside spying on you at home, someone may spy on you at work. Yet the fact that your employer owns the workplace and is paying for your work and time does not by itself justify clandestine gathering of information about you.

The right to privacy is important for a number of reasons. First, it can, in some circumstances, be justified by the principle of fidelity. If it is mutually understood that a work evaluation is private, fidelity requires the employer to guard the disclosure of that information. Second, if violations of privacy violate your desires, they may also violate the principle of autonomy. Third, violations of privacy often violate the principle of harm, causing embarrassment, loss of prestige, or even loss of a job. Moreover, the feeling that you can maintain your own privacy is essential to your attitude toward life. Violations of privacy can be seriously damaging to your sense of pride, self-esteem, and security. Finally, the right to privacy is essential for the protection of other moral rights such as the right to own property, to think freely, to act freely, to pursue happiness, and to speak freely. Environments and societies that ignore people's privacy invariably infringe on these important moral rights.

The Right to Free Expression

The right to free expression is the right to express your own opinion without being penalized for doing so. It is not, however, the right to harm your employer by speaking your mind. An employer may justifiably demote or even fire an employee who repeatedly or purposefully does significant harm to a company. The right to freedom of expression includes the right not to be penalized merely because you said something that displeases your employer. In order for penalties to be justified, the effect of your statements must cause (at least potentially) significant and unjustified harm to the employer.

To become an employee is generally to agree to perform your work to a certain level of productivity. To interfere with that productivity is objectionable on two grounds. First, it violates the work contract between employer and employee. Second, it damages the goals of the employer. It is for these reasons that an employer may be justified in taking reprisal against employees who make statements that irresponsibly damage their employers' interests.

It is the effects of your stated opinions, not their content alone, which may justify reprisal. Of course, divulging technical corporate secrets to outsiders may justify your being fired. Such secrets are essential to successful company business and it is your duty to realize this, so you should maintain them as confidential. If you violate the policies of your employer, this may warrant the employer's response on the grounds that you have proven to be no longer trustworthy.

Suppose, however, that a company has a policy that no employees are to state their political opinions at work. If such a policy is not essential for the success of the company, violating it may do no significant harm to the company's business. In such a case, the policy itself violates the employees' right to free expression.

Justified by the principles of harm and autonomy, the right to free expression is essential for the right to pursue happiness and other important rights. This right is fundamental for any democratic society. It should not be denied at the workplace unless that denial is essential to furthering the legitimate purposes of the employer.

The Right to Due Process

In the workplace, the right to due process is the right of an employee to appeal a decision by management to an impartial third party with the power to correct a wrong. The group empowered to render a decision must be composed of people who do not stand to gain or suffer from the decision. And there must be appropriate procedures to guarantee that the employee receives a fair hearing.

The right to due process protects employees against the arbitrary use of managerial power. Many commercial workplaces take no steps to guarantee this right. Employees who want due process must then appeal to the civil courts. However, civil procedures are slow and cumbersome, and their disadvantages often discourage those who have been wronged from seeking redress. As a result, many unions have established practices of arbitration that protect employees accordingly. Many governments require both government-paid employees and those of government contractors to implement appropriate procedures.

Due process at the workplace is sometimes considered an ethical right for a number of reasons. First, recognition of this right is necessary to protect all the rights and moral rules just mentioned. The extent to which they are important is the extent to which due process is, too. Second, it is based on a combination of the principles of autonomy and harm. Employees are not the property of employers but are autonomous people with the right to pursue happiness as long as it does not infringe on the similar pursuit by others. Employees can be wronged by unjust treatment. Due process gives employees the chance to seek justice when an employer has acted unfairly or arbitrarily. Third, people have a right to some influence over the decisions that affect them. They have a right to protection from arbitrary power over their lives and to work in environments in which there is a balance of certain powers. Fourth, businesses are licensed by society to provide services and products that benefit society. Businesses should and do implement the values of society and should not be allowed to create their own despotic subcultures.

Although some business managers have opposed the formal recognition of the right to due process in the workplace, few have advocated that their own superiors should have unlimited power over them. The principle of equal consideration of interests is one foundation of the right to due process at the workplace. Those who oppose recognition of this right do so largely for the sake of their own benefit.

The Right to Safety

Employees have a right to a workplace in which reasonable precautions have been taken to protect them from bodily harm. What counts as "reasonable precaution" is, of course, not easy to state. However, certain general factors should be considered. Employees should be informed of known risks, encouraged to take care to avoid them, and trained in ways of doing so. But there are difficult questions of degree. How thoroughly employees should be educated and how much care they should take are matters requiring much consideration. These important questions must be answered in the contexts of varying workplaces, and as a result of more detailed and lengthy analysis than is appropriate in this book. However, that there is some basic right to safety is an important ethical consideration based firmly on principles of harm, autonomy, and fidelity, and also many other rights.

The Right to Own Property

Your right to own property is first of all the right to have an extensive degree of control over something you have acquired. You must have acquired the object legitimately in order to have a right to own it. Legitimacy is usually defined by the laws and customs of a given society. Within our society, you have a right to own something only if you have not violated laws of ownership and acquisition (including civil law, antitrust laws, tax laws, laws prohibiting insider trading, cheating in various ways, and so forth).

The degree of freedom you may have in controlling, using, or selling your property varies with the laws of a given society. There are many legal constraints on ownership. To own a gun is not to have the legal or moral right to shoot people; to own a car is not to be justified in driving it at full speed on public highways; to own a house in a city is not to be able to drill for oil legally in your back yard. Furthermore, to own may obligate you to pay taxes. Ownership has perhaps never implied an absolute, unqualified right to control.

The question of which legal constraints on ownership are fair or justified continues to be disputed. Some people argue that the right to own justifies the right of management to exercise almost complete and total power over production, employees, and company policies of all kinds within the law. They maintain that businesses in one country cannot compete successfully on world markets unless managers have extensive powers ensuring flexibility in business practices.

Workers, on the contrary, argue that there must be limits on the power of management. They maintain that workers have certain moral rights—to safety, privacy, freedom of expression, and due process—that justify such limits. Yet some managers maintain that the realities of a free and open job market are enough constraint on management's power. Managers who fail to respect the well-being of employees will lose them to the competition.

The right to own property is important for many reasons. It is a fundamental part of the principle of autonomy, because your autonomy would be severely limited if your right to control your body and your acquisitions were denied. Limitations on the right to own are usually also limitations on the right to trade with others, the right to pursue happiness, and the right to freedom of expression. Moreover, certain negative consequences accrue in any society that imposes severe limitations on its citizens' right to own. The former Soviet Union serves as a case in point. The Communist party instituted such limitations in order to eliminate the exploitation of the laboring class. The resulting restrictions were so severe, however, that they diminished the motivation of many people to excel at work. Moreover, people were largely discouraged from taking risks at work or in business. This ultimately led to social and economic stagnation. Each society must strike a balance between (1) the amount of individual freedom allowed by the right to own and (2) other benefits to society that result from limitations on that right.

The Right to Make a Profit

The right to own is often cited to justify the right of company owners and investors to make a profit from a business enterprise. Those who put forth and thus risk their own resources deserve the benefits of the venture. Their employees are hired on the basis of contractual agreements and deserve to have their contracts fulfilled. However, so the argument goes, whatever funds are left over after these contracts and other expenses are paid are profits and belong properly to the owners and investors. If a business enterprise fails, it is the investors who suffer the burden of losing their resources. Employees lose their jobs, but are free to find employment elsewhere. Because investors back business enterprises for the explicit purpose of making a profit, and take considerable risks in doing so, they have a right to the profits that accrue.

Persuasive as such reasoning may be, there are limits to the right to make a profit. Governments routinely tax business profits and for reasons widely thought to be justifiable. Businesses exist at the discretion of government and for the benefit of society. Tax revenues may be used to benefit society in ways that businesses otherwise would not benefit society. These revenues may be used to maintain a business

environment that fosters competition and thus promotes socially bene-
ficial business activities. Moreover, business practices that are judged
not to benefit society may, as a result, be regulated, limited, or outlawed.
The right to make a profit is thus widely thought to be justifiably limited
by the well-being of society.

The right to make a profit is not widely thought to justify violations
of other ethical principles. Such principles serve to protect human well-
being in general. If the existence of business and the generation of
profits are justified by their benefits to society, then they should take
place within the limits of major ethical principles.

Just what practices are justified by the right to make a profit is
somewhat controversial. Some have argued that this right justifies any
practices consistent with established laws. Such a position assumes
that political pressure alone determines what is right and wrong, or
justifiable and unjustifiable. Others have argued that businesses cannot
prosper and thus produce their full benefit for society unless they are
given the freedom to carry on as competition allows. This position
assumes that the existence of competition will prevent businesses from
doing unjustifiable harm. The lessons of history may offer grounds for
objecting to both assumptions.

Whether the right to make a profit justifies harsh employment
practices is an issue of long-standing debate. How harsh such practices
may be, while still ethically justifiable, is no easy question. Such issues
are worth far more consideration than is appropriate here. In any case,
limitations on the right to own may well extend to the right to make
a profit. Both rights seem justifiably limited by considerations of what
upholds other major ethical principles on the one hand, and the well-
being of society on the other.

The Rights of Future Generations

There are many reasons why it is wrong to pollute the earth and its
atmosphere. One controversial view is that it violates the rights of
future generations, or our duties to them. There has been growing
support in recent years for the thesis that we owe our successors a planet
in which they can make a living and in which we have not destroyed
the natural order beyond repair. This view is based firmly on the
principle of harm and is a part of the principle of fidelity.

If this thesis is correct, future generations may be said to have
certain limited rights. We may not owe them any oil that is now in the

ground, or the continued coexistence of certain species such as the spotted owls of the old-growth forests of the U.S. Northwest. They may be able to live well without the presence of such resources. But it seems clear to many that we do owe them a planet in which they will not be forced to starve and in which the human race is not reduced to extinction due to our carelessness. This right of theirs and duty of ours has extensive implications for institutional policies and individual decisions in our workplaces. In the view of growing numbers of people, the well-being of the earth should now be the single greatest concern of each and every human being.

☐ 2.5 Justice

Justice is embodied in the idea of fairness to all. All versions of justice purport to implement the principle that similar cases should receive similar treatment, or that equals should be treated equally. Because all people have equal value in a fundamental moral sense, everyone should be treated justly. All should be recognized as having to an equal extent the moral rights just listed and should be treated in accord with the moral rules. Justice demands the moral treatment of all in accord with the principle of equal consideration of interests.

There are four main kinds of justice. *Procedural justice* includes the equal chance of all people to receive a fair hearing in any disputes. Procedures designed to implement due process are attempts to implement procedural justice. This kind of justice is fundamental to a just, democratic society and is essential for a humane workplace.

Compensatory justice is the justice of decisions designed to compensate people who have been harmed by others. If you have been fired unjustly, slandered, or robbed, you might appeal to a court of law for compensation. The awarding of monetary damages by that court would be an attempt to implement compensatory justice. The court would seek to determine the harm to the plaintiff and the monetary or other reparations necessary to restore you to your former state of well-being. In order to treat equals equally, the court would compare similar cases to determine the level of appropriate compensation.

Retributive justice is fairness and uniformity in punishment. If you have done wrong and deserve to be punished, the punishment should be fair, appropriate, and similar to fair punishment for similar wrongs by others. Retributive justice is an old concept, repudiated by some who argue that retribution itself cannot be rationally justified. Retribution is the belief that people who do wrong deserve to suffer simply *because* they did wrong. The demand "an eye for an eye and a tooth for a tooth" expresses this ancient idea. Opponents argue that two wrongs cannot make a right and that harming a wrongdoer is merely another wrong deed.

Opponents of retributive justice also argue that only four considerations can justify fines and other penalties. They may be justified by the need to deter others from doing similar wrongs, to prevent a wrongdoer from doing further wrongs, to protect others from further harm the perpetrator is likely to commit, or to educate the perpetrator about the wrongness of the deed. But none of these justify retribution, and thus none of them prove that a culprit deserves to suffer, so it is argued. This viewpoint has become increasingly popular during the twentieth century, and must be considered whenever questions of penalties arise.

Distributive justice pertains to the distribution of goods and services in a society. Here, questions of equality are the source of a fundamental dispute that has traditionally defined the main positions on the political spectrum. People who are referred to as occupying the left end of the spectrum, and known as *socialists,* maintain that society exists in order to benefit its members. Because the lives of all people have equal ethical value, all people have equal ethical rights. It is the role of government to guarantee equal rights for everyone. Democratic socialists believe that these rights are best protected by democratic governments that take strong steps to ensure that in the making of governmental decisions, all people and all parts of society have an equal say and equal power.

Because the lives of all people have equal ethical value, it is the job of government to ensure that everyone has the basic necessities for a decent life. These include minimally decent food, clothing, shelter, health care, education, transportation, and the opportunity for legal redress. In addition, socialists favor government support of institutions promoting individual fulfillment such as libraries and parks. Many favor government sponsorship of the arts and organized sports to ensure access to them by all members of society.

In the view of socialists, the greatest threat to society is the exploitation of the poor by the rich. Democratic socialists seek to limit the political power that can be exercised by the rich, and tend to favor participatory democracy, when feasible. Socialists maintain that the rights to own and to make a profit are not as important as the rights of all members of society to lead a rewarding life. Therefore, government should ensure that the rich do not have too much control over the economy and political institutions of society. The government should maintain careful controls on the marketplace and ensure that economic activities benefit all in society. Such a rationale may lead government to levy heavy taxes on businesses, to regulate prices, and to ensure that workers have power over management decisions that affect them. It may lead to government ownership of industries in transportation, health care, and public utilities.

Those on the right end of the spectrum, known as *libertarians,* view ethical rights as options, maintaining that only ethical rights are properly equal among all people. Everyone has an equal right to participate freely in trading, and thus the marketplace. But individuals' success in the market may differ, and should be allowed to differ. The right to own should be interpreted broadly, so that people are allowed to keep whatever profits they have legally acquired or have been given by those who have legally earned them. Moreover, government should provide people with nothing beyond what they obtain in these two ways.

Representative democracy should protect people from being harmed or enslaved, and enforce whatever rules are needed to maintain a free market economy. Libertarians hold that it is not the responsibility of society to take care of those who fail in the marketplace. The plight of some does not justify taking from those who have been successful. It is not the fault of successful people that some others are unsuccessful. The wealthy should not have their possessions confiscated by government and redistributed to the poor. It may well be that individuals should help others in need, but to do so is not the role of government.

Democratic government should play a minimal role in the life of society, doing little more than maintaining a police force, a military, and a system of courts. But government should not redistribute goods and services. They can be most efficiently and justly distributed in society by private, profit-making capitalist enterprises.

Close to the middle of the political spectrum are liberal and conservative views of distributive justice in a democratic society. The *conservatives* are located a little to the right and the *liberals* a little to the left of center. Liberals maintain that the equality central to the concept of justice includes both rights and, within rather moderate limits, goods and services. They hold that those who are rich are freer than those who are not, and that society should strive to provide a certain minimum degree of equal freedom for all. They favor the existence of a free market, but believe that it is best for all in society that no one be allowed to perish from extreme misfortune or poverty. Therefore, they favor redistributing to the poor some of the excess wealth of the rich. Such redistributions should, however, permit the rich to remain relatively rich. The distributions should provide a minimally decent life for the poor, including a decent minimum level of freedom and opportunity for them. They should receive what is determined by the political process of a representative democracy as necessary to make it possible for one to lead a rewarding life. In most of the developed, capitalist democracies during the late twentieth century, this has come to include food, clothing, shelter, education, health care, transportation, and legal redress. Liberals generally hold that such goods and services should be provided to the poor to a lesser degree than socialists advocate. Like socialists, liberals tend to favor government leadership in providing certain goods and services that enrich life for all members of society. They have favored government establishment of parks, libraries, and an infrastructure including systems for sewage, drinking water, roads, and public transportation. Liberals favor government support of such institutions to a lower level than socialists.

Liberals are less interested than socialists in limiting the economic or political power of the rich. Government should, of course, take a little of the wealth of the rich to support the poor. But beyond this, the rich should be largely free to use their wealth as they choose, as long as it does not interfere with constitutional representative democracy. Moreover, the rich should be free to operate their businesses as they choose, as long as doing so does not violate basic political rights guaranteed by the constitution and the laws of a representative democracy.

The conservative view of distributive justice, a little to the right of center, maintains that all important moral rights can be maintained even though one is poor. According to the conservative position, the wisdom of the ages shows that poverty does not diminish human dignity. It is not the job of government to ensure that everyone has sufficient means to live. Rather, the job of government is to maintain the openness and freedom of the marketplace, preventing monopolies from taking over and protecting individuals from being harmed by others. To do this, government should maintain a few public institutions, such as a system of law enforcement and courts, and public education. Conservatives have come to accept government responsibility for parks, and for maintaining the infrastructure consisting of roads, sewage, and drinking water, although they favor less government support of such institutions than do those on the left.

The job of government is not, for conservatives, to ensure the survival of the poor or homeless. However, recognizing that starvation is not a pretty sight, conservatives have increasingly tended to grant that society may, if it can afford to do so, choose to provide a "social safety net" for unfortunate people who have lost their jobs. This should be a small and temporary allotment of very basic goods and services, provided to help them while they re-establish their places in the market, thus searching to sell their labor or products. The social safety net advocated by conservatives is a smaller allocation of goods and services to the poor than that advocated by liberals, and its purpose is temporary assistance.

Conservatives and liberals both maintain that society should provide for all its citizens an equal opportunity to enter the marketplace of labor, goods, and services. Opportunities should be provided for all citizens to obtain education, and job positions in the government should be nondiscriminatory. However, conservatives differ from liberals in their view of those who do not, for whatever reason, take advantage of educational opportunities and do not gain satisfactory qualifications for a job. Conservatives and libertarians hold that this is no fault of society and that government should take no further steps to benefit such unfortunate people.

Liberals and socialists maintain that equal treatment of citizens implies that government should provide extra opportunities for those who do not take full advantage of educational opportunities to establish employment qualifications. Moreover, liberals and socialists argue that nondiscriminatory government hiring policies do not go far enough to eliminate racial, gender, and other kinds of discrimination. All organizations should take positive steps, or affirmative action, to encourage applications from and seek out job candidates from certain groups that have traditionally been discriminated against in society. This requires, in the view of some liberals, that employers hire women and minority members who are at first unqualified and train them on the job.

Liberals and socialists on the left differ from conservatives and libertarians on the right regarding many other issues. In the main, these differences are based on disagreement over the question of whether poverty and lack of social and economic opportunity unduly restrict human rights, liberty, and dignity. Those on the right argue that history proves that a life of poverty does not necessarily diminish human rights, human liberty, or dignity. Those on the left argue that social realities prove that human rights, liberty, and dignity are significantly diminished in a life of poverty.

☐ 2.6 Self-Interest

Self-interest is not often thought of as an ethical principle. An ethical principle must be consistent with the principle of equal consideration of interests, which imposes a limitation on self-interest. This principle demands that you pursue your self-interest only to the extent that doing so does not treat the interests of others as less important than your own. However, even granting that limitation, self-interest may have a certain ethical justification. You may act in ways properly described as disrespectful to yourself, by abusing your body; you may be said to have duties to yourself.

There are reasons to believe that you have an ethical duty to take care of yourself. First, to fail to do so is to act in a way that impoverishes a small part of society: yourself. Second, a society in which people ignore their duties to themselves would soon disintegrate and its members die off. Third is the fact that most people are happiest, in their most well-adjusted emotional states, when they take care of themselves. Fourth is the argument from tradition. As weak as it may be, it is none the less worth considering. This is the argument that values that have stood the test of time must have some real importance.

One approach to the argument from tradition is known as the *principle of conservatism*. This is the principle, embodied in the law, that you should not interfere with an ongoing practice unless there is clearly good reason to do so. The mere fact that an ongoing practice may be doubted or may have disadvantages, is not sufficient to warrant interference with it. The burden of proof is on the critic to establish that altering the practice will do more good than following it. It is not the responsibility of those who favor the practice to establish its worth. The mere fact that it has persisted to become tradition does count as one significant reason to think that it has some value. People who want to change the practice can be justified in doing so only if they can provide enough reason to believe that the alteration truly does have more benefits.

One universal, traditional, ongoing practice of human beings is to teach their young to take care of themselves and to pursue their own self-interest. Moreover, responsibilities to yourself are embodied in all the teachings of all the great religions of the world, thus expressing the considered judgment of humankind over the ages. These offer significant reason to think that the pursuit of self-interest—as long as it does not contradict the principle of equal consideration of interests—is an ethical, fit, and proper endeavor for human beings.

☐ 2.7 The Network of Ethical Value

It is important to recognize that the ethical principles presented here are all interrelated in meaning, in their import for our lives, and in their justifications. These principles or values may be thought of as related in the form of a network, each intersection of lines an ethical principle connected to the others directly or indirectly. Ethical values are not neat, isolated units that can be adopted or ignored at will. Rather, each one has extensive implications for others. To develop an understanding of one principle often leads to further insights regarding others.

What is common to each of the principles, and what may be thought of as the material constituting the strands of the network, is the principle of equal consideration of interests (ECI). That is, someone who follows the other principles carefully will generally be acting in a way that treats the interests and well-being of others as having as much importance as his or her own. If this principle may be thought of as defining the ethical point of view, each of the other principles helps us in applying that point of view to concrete, specific situations.

It is not clearly helpful or accurate to represent ethical principles as related in an hierarchical manner, as if some were fundamentally or universally more important than others. It is true that ECI is implemented by the other principles, and is, in one sense, more general and fundamental than they. But ECI is not, practically speaking, more important. That is, in specific situations ethical people do not usually find that ECI conflicts with other principles, or that these principles should yield to it. Rather, conflicts of ethical value are usually defined by reference to the other principles. The ethical resolution of such conflicts ordinarily implements ECI in the best way possible.

The network of value is perhaps best viewed as having considerable elasticity. The term "elasticity" refers to the relationship of the various principles in different concrete situations. In some situations, two or more principles may be closely intertwined such that a given decision may violate several at once. In others, a decision may violate only one principle. In one situation, the best decision may be one that upholds one principle but violates another; in another situation, the best decision may do the exact opposite.

Taken together, the principles in the network of ethical value comprise what is sometimes referred to as an ethical world view. They offer counsel on a wide variety of life's problems. Most people who advocate and live by some of these values also accept others. At the basis of every society is broad agreement among many people on most of these values.

The list of ethical principles discussed here is certainly not exhaustive. However, any expansion of this list would likely include the addition of principles and concepts that are partially defined and justified by reference to those just described.

The ethical principles presented here need not be viewed as beyond question. None of them need be viewed as absolute or unexceptionable. The preceding statements of them have limitations and might perhaps be justifiably reformulated for various purposes. The importance of these principles lies not in their lack of exceptions but in their implications for pursuing a good life.

Members of the same society tend to agree broadly on the content of major ethical principles such as those presented here. Most disagreement over ethical issues arises in applying such principles to specific situations. In the case of the hidden cameras, for example, do the maintenance employees have a right to know about the cameras? The answer to such a question depends largely on matters that are specific to the case.

Indeed, some of the most important and challenging work in ethics occurs in the application of these ethical principles to specific, concrete, day-to-day situations. This is the challenge of personal ethical conflicts. The next chapter offers an explanation of the RESOLVEDD strategy of decision making and a sample analysis of the case of the hidden cameras, which applies some of the values explained here.

CHAPTER 3

❑　❑　❑　❑　❑　❑　❑

The RESOLVEDD Strategy of Ethical Decision Making

❑ 3.1 Introduction

The RESOLVEDD strategy is a way of thinking through a personal ethical conflict in order to arrive at the best decision you can. The best decision is one that upholds your most important values to the greatest extent possible in the situation at hand, all things considered. Because your ethical values are some of your most important values, the best decision is an ethical decision, one that upholds these values to the greatest extent possible.

An ethical decision is one that upholds the principle of equal consideration of interests. That is, it is one that treats the interests or well-being of others as being at least as important as your own. If an ethical decision violates any ethical principles, it does so only in order to uphold some other ethical principles that are more important in the case. One important goal in ethical decision making, then, is to determine which ethical principles or values are the most important in the case at hand.

An ethical decision is normally a decision on which you would be willing to stake your reputation. It is one that you think is right on the basis of ethical principles that you try to follow, and that you believe others should follow. It is a decision that you believe is right for good people to make in such cases.

Ethical decisions are usually decisions in which you can take pride. Knowing that you have tried in earnest to apply your ethical principles honestly, you believe you have done your best to be a good person in

35

the situation at hand. You can identify with the decision you have made, believing it is a decision that is suitable for a good person. Your conscience is at peace, and you are ready to enact the decision and live with its consequences.

At times none of this is easy, none of the available options are clearly ethical, and the consequences of the apparently best solution are unfortunate. Herein lies the challenge of ethical decision making. Sometimes there are no simple solutions. The RESOLVEDD strategy does not remove the difficulties of ethical decision making. However, it can help you to clarify those difficulties, to examine them from several perspectives, and to make a well-informed choice.

❏ 3.2 An Overview of the RESOLVEDD Strategy

In brief, the RESOLVEDD strategy includes the following steps:

The RESOLVEDD Strategy

Step 1. *R* REVIEW the history, background, and details of the case.

Step 2. *E* ESTIMATE the conflict or problem present in the case.

Step 3. *S* List the main possible SOLUTIONS to the case.

Step 4. *O* State the important and probable OUTCOMES or consequences of each main solution.

Step 5. *L* Describe the LIKELY IMPACT of each main solution on people's lives.

Step 6. *V* Explain the VALUES upheld and those violated by each main solution.

Step 7. *E* EVALUATE each main solution and its outcomes, likely impact, and the values upheld and violated by it.

Step 8. D_1 DECIDE which solution is the best; state it, clarify its details, and justify it.

Step 9. D_2 DEFEND the decision against objections to its main weaknesses.

In Step 1, to make a decision in accord with the RESOLVEDD strategy, first REVIEW the case at hand, noting the context and background of the case, its origin, and important details, and reflecting on the ethical issues pertinent to the case. In Step 2, formulate an initial grasp or ESTIMATE of the ethical conflict at hand. The understanding you gain in this estimation may later change as you develop the analysis. These initial steps lay the groundwork for the following considerations.

In Step 3, you identify the main possible SOLUTIONS to the case. Before stating these main solutions, you may start with a list of many possible solutions and then group them together, simplifying and narrowing down the list to a more manageable size. The initial multitude of variations of these main solutions may become important later, in the seventh and eighth steps. The next three steps will develop a sustained analysis of the main solutions as they are formulated in the third step.

In Step 4, you identify the main, most likely, and most important possible OUTCOMES or consequences of each main solution. Consider the question "If I choose Solution A, the following things might happen," and then go on to list them. Answers to this question will ordinarily lead you to address considerations that constitute part of the fifth step.

It is especially important, from the ethical point of view, to consider and state (Step 5) the LIKELY IMPACT of each main solution on people's lives. Will a solution likely hurt or help people, and in what ways? The fourth and fifth steps provide information that is essential to the analysis of the case you will develop in later steps. These fourth and fifth steps suggest to you, rather naturally, the ethical principles upheld and violated by each main solution.

In Step 6, you explain and clarify the main VALUES or ethical principles at issue in each main solution. The task here is to clarify which values or principles are upheld and which are violated by each main solution. Simply naming these principles is not enough. It is essential in this step to explain just how and why each main solution violates or upholds these principles.

Up to this point, you have taken stock of the case, noted the main options, listed the important outcomes and likely impact of each, and clarified the values at stake. Now (Step 7) it is time to EVALUATE the main solutions, to compare and contrast them, to determine which are better, which worse, and why. In this seventh step, you make value judgments about the seriousness of the violations of values and the importance of upholding the values described in Step 6. That is, you state your own views on the nature and significance of the ethical issues and present your reasons for holding these views. You explain why some outcomes are more likely to occur than others, some likely impacts of main solutions are more significant than others. This seventh step may well be the longest, most involved, and difficult of all. It requires you to take a stand on various issues, to formulate reasons for your opinions, and to question and evaluate them.

As you work through Step 7, you will eliminate some main solutions from further consideration. You will have formulated arguments to justify your value judgments and conclusions. Your work in this step will be drawing to a close when you have eliminated all but one main solution.

It is important to realize that you may think of new possible solutions as you pursue Step 7. You may discover that you had neglected an option early on and that it offers considerable promise. It is important to maintain an open mind to the possibility that the solutions you identified earlier in the analysis do not exhaust all the possibilities. In-depth analysis in this step may well lead you to a new possible solution that turns out to be the best decision.

The point at which it becomes clear that you favor a particular main solution is the point at which Step 8 begins. This is the step in which you develop and support your DECISION. A number of things need to be done in this step. First, refine your preferred main solution and describe the specific course of action you think is best. The details of your decision are important. You can't determine whether the decision will really work unless you consider these details carefully. Second, explain why you favor the main solution that you do, and why it is ethically preferable to the others. Third, examine the specific course of action you have decided on and show why you think it will work and why it accomplishes the goals you seek in the case. Fourth, justify your view that this specific decision is the best one in the case, taking all important values, outcomes, and other considerations into account.

Step 9 is to DEFEND your decision against the main objections to it. Whether or not you have formulated the perfect decision, someone else may be inclined to cite one or more significant weaknesses of your decision. Your job in this step is to state and explain these weaknesses and defend your decision against it. That is, you need to explain why your decision is still the best one, despite the alleged disadvantages or weaknesses of it.

In presenting the RESOLVEDD strategy, we describe the parts of the strategy as steps. This description is not entirely accurate. Although you may carry out each part of the strategy in the order just presented, you need not always do so. Some of the steps can be mixed in with the others appropriately. Thus, you may do some evaluations immediately after listing some outcomes or likely impacts of main solutions and after clarifying the values upheld and violated by main solutions. But it would be jumping the gun to cover Step 8, your decision, before stating, analyzing, and evaluating the main solutions, their outcomes, likely impacts, and value implications. There are important reasons why the parts of the analysis are suggested in the order they are, but this order need not be viewed as rigid and unalterable.

☐ 3.3 Applying the RESOLVEDD Strategy to the Case of the Hidden Cameras

A description of the case of the hidden cameras is found on page 1. What follows is an analysis of this case as developed by some of our students. Although there is far more to be said about the case than is included in this analysis, it does illustrate an application of the RE-SOLVEDD strategy. The steps of this analysis are in the following order:

Review the case.
Estimate the conflict.
State Solutions 1, 2, and 3
State Outcomes 1 (outcomes of Solution 1)
Suggest Likely Impact 1 (likely impact of Solution 1)
State Values 1 (values upheld and violated by Solution 1)
Outcomes 2 (outcomes of Solution 2)
Likely Impact 2 (likely impact of Solution 2)
Values 2 (values upheld and violated by Solution 2)
Outcomes 3 (outcomes of Solution 3)
Likely Impact 3 (likely impact of Solution 3)
Values 3 (values upheld and violated by Solution 3)
Evaluation
Decision
Defense

A RESOLVEDD Analysis of the Case of the Hidden Cameras

Review   Hidden cameras are objectionable for a number of reasons. First, since they are hidden, they may pick up employee conversations and actions that are potentially embarrassing or immoral, even if not illegal. Second, there are many questions about what may be done with the information gained. Will it sit in a file or on a tape somewhere, waiting to be used by some administrator at the right time? What counts as the right time, and who will decide? Who will safeguard access to this information, and how well? All these issues need careful attention in order for hidden cameras to avoid the violation of important ethical values. Third, since the cameras are hidden and unknown by employees, students, and others, their very presence violates the right to privacy. These people believe they have privacy; in fact, they do not. Fourth, employees have no right to due process regarding the information gained by the cameras until their presence is exposed. One cannot complain about such information unless one knows it exists. Fifth, hidden cameras involve deception if those under surveillance believe they are not being observed. To this extent, such cameras would violate the trust of employees, students, and others.

Estimation   This is a touchy issue for a summer employee. Because I have worked in this job for only two weeks, I am low person on the totem pole. I can be fired for almost any reason at all, or perhaps for no reason. If I decide to object further about the cameras, I may have to face the consequences. Yet I am in a weak position to see the whole thing through, because resolution of the issue may take months. And in about two months I will be back in college, tied down by homework and additional work, and impoverished by a lack of summer earnings if I were to lose my job.

My problem arises from the fact that I am now convinced that the cameras should not be installed without proper safeguards, and without employee knowledge of them. Because I have already complained to the superintendent, I have nowhere further to go but outside the school administration, possibly exposing the cameras. Moreover, I am personally afraid of stirring up such a controversy, possibly damaging my reputation in the local area and appearing to be an untrustworthy busy-body. How will I ever get another job locally?

Ethically, my problem is whether I have a stronger duty to my employer or to other school employees, students, and others, including society.

Solutions   My main options in the case are to (1) ignore the whole issue and quietly install the cameras, telling no one; (2) refuse to complete the installation of the cameras; or (3) complain to the board of education or the newspapers.

Outcomes 1   If I quietly install the cameras, the culprits may be caught, or the hidden cameras may be discovered by other workers and an uproar may occur. But I might not be implicated by the whole thing and may never hear of it again.

Likely Impact 1   If I quietly install the cameras, the private or personal lives of school employees, students, and others may be compromised. Whatever happens, it may eventually come out that I was the one who installed the cameras, and my reputation may be damaged accordingly.

Values 1   Quietly installing the cameras would uphold the principle of fidelity to my employer by following the initial agreement I made and my boss's instructions. It would also uphold the principle of confidentiality by keeping the job-related information under control. It would protect the autonomy of the school administrators, their rights to try to catch the culprits, and the right of the school to own and control its property. It would, moreover, also uphold the principle of harm by not interfering in the school's effort to protect itself.

Quietly installing the cameras would violate the principles of fidelity and harm toward my fellow workers because I would be an accomplice to the administration's violation of their rights to privacy, due process, and nondeceptive treatment as explained in the review step.

Outcomes 2   The second solution, refusing to complete the installation of the cameras but not complaining further, might keep me out of trouble. If my boss thinks well of me, she would probably not fire me for changing my mind. Furthermore, she might be afraid that if she did, I might expose the hidden cameras to the newspapers. The outcomes of such a solution would be that the cameras would likely be installed by someone else, and my name would escape connection with them.

Likely Impact 2   The second solution, signing off the job, would be easy on my boss and the administration and easy on me. But I would be allowing the hidden cameras to be installed and permitting them to have negative effects on the lives of school employees, students, and others.

Values 2   Quietly refusing to complete the installation would uphold the principle of confidentiality to my employer, the autonomy of school administrators, their rights to try to catch the culprits, and the right of the school to own and control its property, much as the first solution would do. Although I would be begging off the case, I would leave the administration free to assign someone else to the task. I think that my refusal would not violate the principle of fidelity toward my employer, although it would violate my original agreement to install the cameras. However, when I made that agreement I did not promise or hint that I might not change my mind later. Surely I am free to do so without violating any moral principles.

This second solution does not free me from the responsibilities I violate by the solution of following orders quietly. By begging off the job and doing nothing further, I am still an accomplice in violating the values sacrificed by the presence of the cameras. If I could have taken action to remedy the situation, but did not, then I acquiesce to the violations of the principles of harm and fidelity toward my fellow workers that result from the violations of their rights and well-being by the hidden cameras.

Outcomes 3   The third solution, that of reporting the problem to the newspapers, might result in the culprits discovering the presence of the cameras. My reporting the cameras might thus hamper the school district's efforts to catch the thieves. Yet reporting the problem to the board of education might not have that effect, depending on whether the board discusses the issue in public. Reporting the problem may ensure that the general issue is debated either by those in positions of authority or by the general public.

Likely Impact 3   This third solution would cause major problems for the school administrators, conflict for the school employees, and troubles for me. I might become involved in a long and complicated debate, lose my job, or find my reputation damaged. I would receive few external rewards for pursuing such a solution, and would have to have a strong personal conviction in order to pursue it.

Values 3   If I pursued this solution, I would uphold the principles of harm and fidelity toward my fellow workers, students, and others by upholding their rights to know, to act autonomously, to due process, and to freedom of expression.

This third solution would violate the principles of confidentiality and fidelity toward the school administration by betraying its trust and exposing the confidential information. It would violate the principle of harm toward the administration by preventing it from protecting the equipment and catching the culprits. It would violate the school's right to protect its equipment and safeguard its ownership.

Evaluation　My personal conflict in the case stems from, on the one hand, the rights to privacy, autonomy, and due process of the school employees, students, and others, and on the other hand, the right of the administration to prevent theft and catch the thieves. In my opinion, a person's right to privacy is more important than catching any thieves. Violations of the right to privacy are serious affronts to the spirit of democracy, autonomy, freedom of thought and expression, and trust. They cannot be remedied by something as simple as buying a new VCR. Furthermore, there are other ways to prevent theft than installing hidden cameras that violate privacy and autonomy. Such alternate methods may be expensive and troublesome, but they are worth the cost. The superintendent's right to catch a thief does not give him the right to use any means he chooses to obtain the desired information. To observe employees without their knowing is simply deceptive and violates the rights of the innocent. The school administration has taken the easy way out of a difficult problem and in doing so has sacrificed some fundamental ethical and political values. The end does not always justify the means.

It is worth noting here that both Solutions 1 and 3 are likely to end in compromising my reputation, either by my association with the installation of the cameras or by my reporting them. Only the second solution, that of begging off the case, is likely to relieve me of this association. But this solution is just as ethically objectionable as the first and should be avoided for the same reasons. However, it is clear that a major challenge of this situation is to figure out a way to do the right thing without seriously sacrificing my own personal reputation.

Decision　Because I disagree so strongly with the administration's value judgment in the case, I should act to oppose it. In doing so, however, I will try to find a way to resolve the problem while doing as little damage as possible to the administration's right to protect its property. Telling the newspaper would create a public issue at the expense of that right. But notifying the board of education would not necessarily harm the school district.

I would call up the president of the board, explain the problem, and ask that the board address it. The board would then have the option of discussing it privately or at a public meeting, as it chooses. If it handles the matter quietly, neither confidentiality nor my job nor reputation might suffer. Explaining this to the board president might help avoid a scandal, and everyone affected might be protected. Although I would still have violated the principle of fidelity toward the superintendent and the principal, it is possible that no other significant values would be violated. This is an approach I could live with, knowing that I had done my best under the circumstances.

Defense   There are a number of weaknesses of my decision, though none are important enough to warrant another approach. If the board makes it public and it appears in the newspapers, a public debate could follow. But at least I was not the one to blow it. The board has a right to know about the cameras, and I did not violate confidentiality by notifying the board. I cannot be blamed for any ensuing uproar caused by the board's mishandling of the issue.

One option that I have not yet addressed above is that of floating a rumor about the cameras. This might alert the employees to the risks to their privacy and cause the maintenance employees to inquire about the cameras. By such an approach, I would be acting deceptively and violating both the principles of confidentiality and fidelity to the administration. Moreover, the rumor might be traced back to me, and the thieves might even find out. Such an approach would be egoistically motivated, cowardly, deceptive, and underhanded, and could do more to damage my reputation than the other options.

Another problem with notifying the president of the board is that even if I did not lose my job this year, I would be unlikely to be hired at the job next year. This is a disadvantage I can live with, because I would feel uncomfortable working for this administration again anyway, and I have a full year in which to find another job.

☐ 3.4 Unknown Facts

A description of a personal ethical conflict may make no mention of certain factual information that is relevant to your decision and that you might be aware of if you were actually in similar circumstances. In the case of the hidden cameras, for example, the board of education might have taken a position on such matters, and you might know it. However, such information was not stated in the case description, and you should assume it is not known and is not readily knowable by you during the time you make your decision.

It is important to recognize that most decisions are made in the presence of significant factual uncertainty. There are almost always important facts that decision makers simply do not have. All decisions are based on a degree of speculation. The author of the present analysis speculates on questions of (1) how the superintendent might react to news that the hidden cameras had been leaked to the press and (2) how the president of the board of education might react to the news of the cameras. The author also speculates that the president of the board does not know about the cameras. Decision making in ethics, as in all fields, requires you to respond thoughtfully to the different possibilities regarding unknown facts. Of course, a miscalculation on such questions can lead you to make a decision with disastrous consequences. It is part of the art of effective decision making to learn how to address and work with such uncertainties.

☐ 3.5 Lacking Time

It takes considerable time and concentration to develop an analysis of a personal ethical conflict. Yet such a conflict may occur in a complex situation that demands a quick decision. How can the RESOLVEDD strategy be of help in such high-pressured situations?

There may, of course, be times when you cannot work out a complete RESOLVEDD analysis. In such contexts, you have no choice but to rely on various habits of thought that you have developed in advance. Such habits can be developed by practicing the RESOLVEDD strategy on cases such as those presented in this book.

Practice may help you become more familiar with ethical principles such as those presented in Chapter 2. You may become better able to detect situations in which these principles play important parts. You may be able to determine immediately that a certain possible decision upholds or violates a certain important principle. Such quick grasp of the important ethical factors in a conflict is sometimes described as intuition or insight. Practice in using the RESOLVEDD strategy can help you develop and sharpen your intuitive abilities.

As you develop facility with the RESOLVEDD strategy, you may need less and less time to develop an ethical analysis. You may find that you need less time to cover the more routine steps of the strategy. This, in turn, may give you relatively more time to consider the most trying issues of a conflict.

Practice in applying the strategy may help you establish value judgments that are useful for further ethical conflicts, and that help you reduce the time needed to analyze them. If, in some future case, you face an issue that you addressed earlier, the approach you took before may be applied again, thus saving you further time. Or, a mistake you made earlier may well have taught you a lesson that is of central importance in some future conflict. With increased practice, each new ethical conflict becomes less novel and needs less time for analysis.

There is no denying that the pressures of time can increase the likelihood of making unsatisfactory decisions. It is certainly best to use as much time as possible to address and analyze personal ethical conflicts. By practicing the RESOLVEDD strategy, you may progress from making thoughtful analyses to making better decisions in less time.

❑ 3.6 A Checklist

REVIEW
- What are the particularly important relevant details of the case?
- How did the situation come about?
- Is something wrong? What? Why?
- Is anyone at fault? Why?
- Is there likely to be disagreement over the case from people related differently to it? Why? What are the different perspectives people may have on the case?
- What information would you like to have that is missing and without which you must still decide?

ESTIMATION
- What options do *you* have in the situation?
- Why is it difficult to make a decision in the case?
- Initially, what do you think is the main ethical conflict in the case?
- What main points will you need to consider in making the decision?

SOLUTIONS
- Group the options into a small, manageable number of main solutions.

OUTCOMES
- What are the significant possible outcomes, results, consequences of each main solution?

LIKELY IMPACTS
- What outcomes of each main solution are possible but extremely unlikely, and why?
- In what ways is each main solution (you might implement) likely to affect people's lives?
- In what ways might each main solution hurt or help people?

VALUES
- What important ethical principles are upheld by each main solution, and how are they upheld by it?
- What important ethical principles are violated by each main solution, and how are they violated by it?
- Have you explained how each main ethical principle is violated or upheld by each main solution?

EVALUATION
- Are some consequences of some possible solutions more important than others? Why?
- Does one solution uphold or violate certain values in more or less important ways than another? Why?
- Why is one possible main solution better or worse than another?
- If all main solutions are unsatisfactory, have you searched for other possibilities? Have you considered that new, as-yet-unthought-of possibilities may be hidden in your main solutions, and that you might find a variation of one that is quite satisfactory?

DECISION
- Exactly how will you carry out your decision? Explain the details.
- Just why is this decision the best, all things considered? Explain.

DEFENSE
- What are the main weaknesses of your decision? Why might someone object to your decision?
- If these weaknesses have not been stated and addressed earlier, do so here.
- What are the best answers to these weaknesses? Why do you still think your decision is the best? Explain.

□ □ □ □ □ □ □

CHAPTER 4

Detailed Discussion of the RESOLVEDD Strategy

The preceding chapter offers an initial presentation of the RESOLVEDD strategy and an analysis of the case of the hidden cameras. This chapter addresses, in more depth, some of the issues you confront in developing a RESOLVEDD analysis.

□ 4.1 When Is an Ethical Principle Upheld by a Given Solution?

The mere fact that a given solution does not violate an ethical principle is not proof that the solution upholds the principle. Consider, in the case of the hidden cameras, the solution of complaining no further and simply obeying the orders of the superintendent of schools. Such a solution does not clearly violate the principle of truth, because you are not clearly deceiving anyone. But neither does it uphold that principle. Rather, that principle does not clearly pertain to that solution. It's best, then, simply not to mention that principle in Step 6, the values portion of your analysis.

Consider, however, whether or not the principle of confidentiality is relevant to the solution of following orders. Following your boss's orders and installing the cameras clearly does not violate that principle. But does it uphold that principle, and why or why not?

To answer this question, we must consider the whole case and its alternative solutions. One possible solution is to take your complaint to the newspapers. Doing so certainly would result in your violating the principle of confidentiality. By going to the newspapers, you would release to the public, without permission, certain information to which you had been entrusted in your capacity as an employee. This fact is essential to answering the question. It reveals that the principle of confidentiality is a relevant ethical value in the case and that it may be violated by one possible solution but not by another. Therefore, the solution that does not violate it is ethically better to that extent and for that reason. As a consequence, it is an important fact about the solution of obeying orders that it does not violate the principle of confidentiality. You may point out that fact by indicating that this solution upholds that principle.

The following is a condition that must be present in order for a given ethical principle or value to be upheld by a given solution: For a solution to uphold a value, there must be some other solution to the problem at hand that would violate that value. If a given value is not violated by any possible solution to a personal ethical conflict, then the value need not be mentioned in your analysis. Such a value is neither violated nor upheld by any solution to the conflict and should probably not play any significant role in your analysis.

There may be a possible main solution that violates a certain ethical principle but that is extremely unattractive for various reasons. In such a case, there's no significant reason to state that the alternative solutions uphold this ethical principle. In such a case, this principle is largely immaterial to the decision at hand.

Consider a possible (but outrageous) solution to the case of the hidden cameras. One could decide to assassinate the superintendent of schools! Such a solution would violate the principle of harm to the superintendent. But this hardly justifies your citing as an advantage of the other possible solutions that they uphold the principle of harm by their allowing the superintendent to live! Making such a point is generally unnecessary, because this is such an extremely bad solution on so many grounds. Citing this application of the principle of harm as an advantage of other solutions is unnecessary for someone who is trying to live by the ethical point of view. A second condition for a value to be upheld, then, is that the alternative solution that violates it is worth being considered by an ethical person. These two requirements for a value to be upheld can be combined into one:

For a solution to uphold a value, there must be some significant ethical reason to choose another solution that would violate the value.

☐ 4.2 A Solution Can Uphold and Violate the Same Ethical Principle

It is important to recognize that a given solution to a personal ethical conflict can both uphold a given ethical principle and violate it at the same time. This is possible because of the broad and general nature of major ethical principles. Consider the following solution to the case of the hidden cameras: you decide to install the cameras but inform the maintenance employees about them. By doing so, you may both uphold and violate the principle of fidelity. You uphold it by acting in a way that is faithful to the interests of the maintenance employees, and you violate it by breaking faith with the superintendent. That is, you uphold it in one way and violate it in another.

These considerations help clarify the importance of explaining, in Step 6, the values section, just how a main solution violates a given ethical principle. The important point is not that an ethical principle is violated by a solution. It is the specific way in which it is violated that you must consider in the evaluation of the solution. The mere fact that an ethical principle is violated by a solution does not prove that the solution is ethically wrong. Awareness of such violation is merely awareness of one reason to think the solution is wrong. But there may be other, more important reasons why it is the best solution given the circumstances. These can only be understood and evaluated by examining the specific way in which the ethical principle is violated.

The ethical principles are general in nature. Each concrete situation pertains to a given principle in a slightly different manner, depending on the particulars of the situation. Ethical decision making requires that one look very carefully into those particulars and understand each situation as a unique instance of the relevant ethical principles. Each instance will embody the ethical value of a principle in its own unique way and to a greater or lesser extent. Your decision must grow out of careful consideration of the ethical value uniquely present in the various alternative main solutions.

☐ 4.3 Understanding the Evaluation Stage

It is important to understand the difference between (1) describing the outcomes, likely impacts, and values upheld and violated by the main solutions, and (2) the evaluation of these three. The evaluation is not simply a summary or a combination of the other steps. It involves some fundamentally different kinds of thinking and is essential for arriving at a well-considered decision.

Statements that are characteristically within the solutions, outcomes, likely impacts, and values steps are all objective, detached, and descriptive in nature. These are statements presenting the basic, ethically relevant facts of the case. They are not statements asserting that you believe that something is right or wrong, good or bad, or has a particular degree of value.

To state as a main solution "I could argue my case to the board of education" is to say that this is a possibility. It is not to state a value judgment regarding how good or bad the solution is. It does not assert that your own values give any reason to think that the solution is good or bad.

To state an outcome or likely impact of a solution is to describe one or more possible consequences of it. It is not to state how important the outcome or likely impact is, whether it is desirable or undesirable, or even how probable it is that such an outcome or likely impact might occur. To indicate your opinions on such matters is to evaluate them.

This distinction between the application of concepts and your own value judgments is pertinent to Step 6, regarding values upheld and violated by a possible main solution. Consider the following: "Presenting my objections to the board of education would violate the principles of confidentiality and harm by making public the confidential information and interfering with the attempt to solve the problem of theft." This statement merely asserts that the solution violates two values. But it does not present your evaluation of these violations. It does not indicate, for example, whether in your view they are ethically insignificant in comparison to other ethical values at stake in the case. The statement does not indicate whether you think the harm done is serious or how serious it is. It does not indicate whether the harm done by going to the board is as serious as the harm that would result from dropping the issue altogether. Nor does it indicate whether you think the violation of confidentiality is ethically justifiable or not. These matters of evaluation need to be stated and supported with reasons, and constitute Step 7 of the process.

To evaluate, then, is to present your opinion of what is right, wrong, good, bad, important, insignificant, or ethically justifiable or unjustifiable. It is to begin to develop your own point of view after you have clarified the facts and principles that are relevant to the case. It requires that you make value judgments and then present and weigh the reasoning, evidence, or considerations that support those judgments. The result of evaluating is that you eliminate certain options from consideration and rank the others in order of preference, given your viewpoint.

❑ 4.4 Avoiding Moral Arithmetic

In the process of evaluating, you may be tempted to take a shortcut that is best viewed as unhelpful and misleading. This is the temptation to count the values upheld and the values violated by each main solution and then to decide that the solution that upholds the largest number of values or violates the smallest number of values, or that upholds the greatest number of net values, is the best. Such a procedure may be described as "moral arithmetic" and is seriously misleading.

To count the number of values upheld and the number violated assumes that each value upheld or violated is of equal importance in both ethical and other relevant ways. This, however, is not always the case. Within a certain situation, for example, a violation of confidentiality may not be as ethically significant as a violation of some other value. Indeed, it is possible that a certain solution could violate one ethical principle while another violates many and that the first solution is still the worse of the two. For example, a case could occur in which the right to life weighs on one side, while honesty, free expression, and the right to own figure on the other. Here, the right to life would be more important than the other three.

❑ 4.5 Moral and Other Ideals Are Rarely Helpful

The discussion of ethical values in Chapter 2 omits consideration of a whole group of important ethical principles. This category has been described by the philosopher Bernard Gert as *moral ideals*.* A moral ideal is an important moral principle by which one seeks to improve the world through reducing the presence of evil. Moral ideals express

---

* The discussion of moral ideals in this section largely follows the work of Bernard Gert, *Morality: A New Justification of the Moral Rules* (New York: Oxford University Press, 1988), Chapter 8.

high values to which some people aspire yet recognize as difficult to live up to. For every moral rule, there is a corresponding moral ideal. For the moral rule that one should not harm people (the principle of harm), there is a moral ideal that you should try to help people (the principle of beneficence) and thus act to relieve pain. For the moral rule that you should not break your promises (the principle of fidelity), there is a moral ideal that you should act to help people resist breaking their promises. For the moral rule that you should not deceive people (the principle of truth), there is a moral ideal that you should act to prevent deception. In general, moral rules require you to avoid doing harm, whereas moral ideals encourage you to try to perform good deeds.

Advocates of a moral ideal take it very seriously, often to the point of believing that it embodies the very highest value to which a human being can aspire. They may even view it as essential to a meaningful life. Moral ideals may be important sources of personal motivation.

Moral ideals may be thought of as defining a moral maximum, while moral rules define a moral minimum. To violate a moral rule is to do something that is, ordinarily, wrong. However, you cannot, properly speaking, "violate" a moral ideal. You may fail to live up to its strong demands and thus fall short of a high and worthy goal. But in doing so you do not necessarily act wrongly. You can sometimes avoid opportunities to help others without actually hurting them. From an ethical perspective, it is bad to hurt people but not always bad not to help them. To this extent, you are ethically required to follow moral rules but not moral ideals.

Although moral ideals may express our highest moral aspirations, they do not necessarily express more important values than moral rules. It may be worse to violate a moral rule than a moral ideal. If it is wrong to murder people, then it may not be justifiable to do so in order to make the world a better place by eliminating a gangster. Acting to uphold a moral ideal ordinarily does not negate the wrong done by violating a moral rule. In the end, a deed that violates a moral rule may do more harm than the amount of good that results from the extent to which the deed upholds a moral ideal.

There are, of course, other kinds of ideals, such as religious or political ideals. Some of the relationships among these other ideals and other corresponding religious, political, and other principles are similar to the relationship among moral ideals and moral rules mentioned here. Consider the Christian ideal expressed in the Golden Rule ("Do unto others as you would want them to do unto you"). Although a Christian believes that people should strive to follow the Golden Rule, Christians generally do not view the failure to do so as being as seriously wrong as murder or stealing (both forbidden by the Ten Commandments).

The case of Lieutenant Colonel Oliver North, the White House attaché for President Reagan, may serve as a case in point. North lied, deceived government officials, and violated government policies and laws in a number of ways during the Iran-Contra affair in the mid-1980s. Throughout the Senate hearings and his trials, he tried to establish that he did these things to serve the best interests of the United States. He tried to dramatize to the nation that he acted on noble motives and had strived to live up to the highest ideals of patriotism. However, few were persuaded by his appeals, and he was, initially, duly convicted on the grounds that the ideal of patriotism was no justification or excuse for violating the law and the moral rules it implements. Few were persuaded that attempts to live up to an important ideal negate, override, or compensate for violations of the law and moral rules and other ethical principles. (North's later acquittals on most charges were based more on legal technicalities than on the view that his patriotism should excuse him.)

There is no denying that religious, moral, or political ideals may be more important for some individuals than their moral rules. However, those who violate moral rules in order to uphold their cherished ideals often seem to do so out of a zealous and partly blind enthusiasm that ends in violating the rights and values of other individuals. Those who seek to uphold an ideal, and in doing so violate a moral rule, are sometimes referred to as *fanatics*.* A fanatic may be described as a person who does what is ethically wrong in order to uphold some ideal or cause in a way that is not ethically justifiable. Although your ideals may be important to you, this should not reduce your respect for the interests of others. The principle of equal consideration of interests (ECI), that we should not treat the interests of others as less important than our own, is of real importance in this context. It is one important basis of all the moral rules, rights, and principles discussed in Chapter 2. Although this is not the place to defend this principle, its importance is clear from the fact that it has been largely supported for the past two centuries, in different formulations, by many of the most important thinkers and writers on ethics. It seems unlikely that ideals provide sound justification for violating ECI.

* Gert, *Morality*, p. 165.

Consideration of moral and other ideals has been deferred until now because they are rarely helpful in resolving personal ethical conflicts. People differ greatly in their interpretations of such ideals and in their views of proper implementation. Such diversity does not prove these ideals to be mistaken or less important. However, the ideals should be treated with caution, and not assumed, without careful consideration, to justify violation of other moral or ethical principles or ECI. Insofar as moral rules, rights, and other values effectively implement ECI, these should be taken very seriously before they are sacrificed to do what seems to follow some moral, religious, political, or other ideal.

There is one kind of situation in which you may find it helpful to consider the extent to which a given decision fulfills one of your important ideals. This may occur when you find that all other ethical considerations in the case are distributed evenly over and thus balanced for and against two or more alternatives. That is, if there is no other compelling reason to do one thing or another, one of your important ideals favors a certain decision, and the application of that ideal in the circumstances is consistent with ECI, then that ideal may offer you good reason to make that decision accordingly.

☐ 4.6 Conscience and Intuitions

Most people who are concerned to try to act ethically have a conscience. To have a conscience is to have the inclination to feel guilty for doing something wrong. A conscience may play an important role in your life, for it is something you probably want to avoid violating.

Your conscience may at times serve you as an indicator of right and wrong. That is, you may sometimes find that you have a clear intuition, feeling, or sense that a certain course of action would be wrong. Such intuitions are useful, as they help us make up our minds in situations when there is too little time and a split-second decision is needed. However, it is important not to rely too heavily on our conscience or intuitions, for they are not fool-proof. Sometimes the content of intuitions and "pangs of conscience" is not clear or coherent, and at other times such hunches are misleading.

Conscience may be thought of as a red flag, a warning sign that perhaps something is not quite right. However, you must still decide for yourself what to do and whether conscience truly does indicate the best course of action. Further reflection and analysis may be needed to determine just what your conscience really does indicate and to determine if the verdict of your conscience or intuitions is correct.

The best way to make a decision is to consider all sides of the case, weigh the import of all possible outcomes, likely impacts on people's lives, and relevant values, and choose accordingly. The RESOLVEDD strategy can help you conduct that investigation on your own, given adequate time. Use of the strategy will likely help you develop your ability to analyze personal ethical conflicts and may thus strengthen your powers of intuition and conscience.

It is important, however, that you do not cite your conscience or intuitions as reasons that favor or oppose a given decision. Conscience and intuitions are vague notions whose apparent content needs to be questioned, analyzed, and evaluated as much as any other voice to which we listen. Use of the RESOLVEDD strategy should sharpen your powers of intuition and conscience and not be guided blindly by them.

❑ 4.7 Defending Your Decision

The last step in your analysis is to state the most significant weakness of your decision and defend your decision against it. The specific nature of a main weakness depends on the particulars of the case. Perhaps one might object that you are overoptimistic in thinking your decision will resolve a certain practical problem in the case. Or perhaps your decision violates some important principle for a less important reason. You may have underrated the odds that a given outcome would materialize or that a person's life would be affected in a certain way. Or you may have overlooked, in your analysis to this point, another solution that might appear to have more advantages than your stated decision.

If you identify an objection that is so serious that you cannot defend your decision adequately, you may need to go back and reconsider some other possible options. You may need to reformulate your decision and possibly even your evaluations. Your task is not finished until you have established, to the best of your ability, that your decision is the best one possible in the case, all things considered.

This final step in the analysis is in many ways the most trying. Once you have formulated your decision and defended it, you may feel rather confident about it, and perhaps even proud that you have come this far and done so well. You may find it emotionally difficult to switch to the role of critic of your own work.

Before taking on the task of critic, it may be helpful to let some time lapse after completing Step 8. Time may help you to gain some perspective on your work, to admit you are human and have limitations, and to grant that others normally and reasonably disagree about many things we do and believe. Such disagreements need not reflect negatively on us. Rather, they may offer valuable insights and encourage us to broaden our own thinking.

Another helpful strategy is to tell someone else about the case and ask for suggestions. Others may offer reflections and perspectives you had not thought of. Their ideas may raise questions you should address. They may help you to maintain a more objective stance toward the case and your analysis. The effort to carry out this ninth step may help you to learn important lessons about yourself, your thinking, and the case at hand.

CHAPTER 5

❏ ❏ ❏ ❏ ❏ ❏ ❏

Two Analyses of Personal Ethical Conflicts

The following two cases describing personal ethical conflicts are accompanied by analyses that apply the RESOLVEDD strategy. In reviewing them, you may find it helpful to identify each of the RESOLVEDD points in the analyses.

❏ 5.1 Treating Toivo Tough

You are a shift manager at Korry Manufacturing, a small firm that makes small parts for large airplane manufacturers. Hourly employees are protected by a union contract, which includes an appeals process and provision for binding arbitration in the case of employer-employee disputes. One of your senior hourly employees, Toivo, is minimally competent and is disliked by management.

Toivo is thought to be too highly paid for the quality and quantity of his work. He operates a punch press, which is a refrigerator-sized machine that shapes a small piece of metal into a part for some mechanism. He produces more than twice the rate of defective parts of any other employee in the firm. You have discussed this with him, complaining about the low quality of his work and offering to provide him counseling, education, and training to help increase his powers of concentration at work. He has, however, largely shrugged off your suggestions, pointing out that no one is perfect and that his work is not unsatisfactory according to union standards.

Other employees recognize his limitations, but seem neither willing nor able to do much about them. He is not the cause of any significant problem in morale, for other workers tend to be amused by him, make him the butt of their jokes, and even seem to like him. Rarely have they grumbled about him in a serious way.

Now in his mid-fifties, Toivo will not likely retire for another decade. His seniority protects him from layoffs during business recessions. Although he is not a major problem for Korry, you have mentioned him to your boss, who has been impressed by the problem. Indeed, he regularly asks you what you are doing to help "shake off that deadwood."

Recently, your boss has suggested quite seriously that you take steps to make work at Korry less palatable for Toivo, thus encouraging him to seek employment elsewhere. Your boss suggests that, as a stimulus, you move him around from one to another of the most undesirable jobs on the production floor. Your boss assures you that such treatment is entirely legal, forbidden neither by the union contract nor other labor laws.

It has been customary at Korry to move production workers around from job to job periodically, thus rotating them in and out of the undesirable jobs. Employees seem to have adjusted well to this arrangement, tolerating these monotonous jobs about as well as can be expected. Management does have the power and legal right, however, to alter these practices.

What should you do in response to the problems posed by Toivo and your boss? Analyze the case until it is RESOLVEDD.

☐ 5.2 An Analysis of "Treating Toivo Tough"

According to the case description, my boss only suggested a solution to the case but did not order it. I am under no clear obligation to do exactly as he suggested. But I do owe it to my employer to try to find a way to raise productivity.

It seems clear that although Toivo's work is below par, it is not substandard and offers no grounds for firing him. He is not really doing anything wrong but is clearly the worst employee I have.

I could (1) do as my boss suggests, rotating Toivo among the most undesirable jobs, or (2) resist my boss's suggestion and handle the case in my own particular way. If I choose this second approach, I have several options. These include my continuing to counsel Toivo, giving him time off to attend training sessions, and persuading the union to put pressure on him.

If I do as my boss suggests and rotate Toivo among the most undesirable jobs on the production floor, my boss might be pleased that I am following his suggestion. But Toivo might figure out what is going on (after all, Toivo is only lazy, not stupid!) and begin to seek ways to stop it. If he took the case to the union, he might win a grievance on the grounds that my strategy is harassment.

Following my boss's suggestion would likely make Toivo quite unhappy. This in turn could backfire on me, if Toivo was successful in gaining the attention and sympathy of his fellow workers. The whole thing could turn into a nasty, demoralizing, and efficiency-reducing labor-management conflict.

Doing as my boss suggests would be a way of upholding the principle of fidelity toward my boss and the company. I would be respecting the chain of command and taking steps to address a personnel problem and increase efficiency. It might be argued that this solution is also best for Toivo if it succeeds in motivating him to shape up or ship out.

This first solution would violate the principle of autonomy toward Toivo. Merely shifting him around to the worst jobs without informing him of my motives would not put him in a position to face the challenge squarely. He might, as a result, become confused and demoralized, without realizing that he does in fact have a choice. Although I would be happy if he were to quit, he does have a right to understand that he need not do so but could shape up instead.

Similarly, this strategy would violate the principle of truth toward Toivo, by hiding my true motives from him. It would violate the principle of fidelity toward Toivo, as I would be acting in a way that is hardly faithful to him and not clearly in his best interests. Rather than helping production run smoothly, this solution would have the single purpose of sabotaging one person and making his life miserable by manipulating him. It would, thus, violate the principle of harm toward Toivo.

If, however, I implement the second solution, ignoring my boss's suggestion and handling the case in my own way, my boss may view me as stubborn and inflexible. This could lead to my receiving a poor job performance review (JPR). But if my own method of handling the case is effective, this might redeem me in the eyes of my boss.

Ignoring my boss's suggestion might be viewed as violating the principle of fidelity toward my boss and employer by ignoring the authority in the chain of command. However, there is some room for debate here, because my boss only made a suggestion, and it is not completely clear that I am expected to follow it as if it were an order.

The main problem with the second solution, ignoring my boss's suggestion, is that doing so would jeopardize my boss's opinion and thus my JPR. It is doubtful that doing so would be any significant violation of the principle of fidelity, as my boss merely suggested but did not order. However, there are grounds for doubting that any effort I make to solve the problem on my own would likely be successful. Given Toivo's personality and my total failure to get him to cooperate so far, it seems unlikely that I will have much luck in my efforts to reform him. Such an approach would be personally risky, even if not ethically problematic.

The first solution, following my boss's suggestion, has serious ethical problems. It would be treating Toivo in an underhanded and nasty way, seriously violating the principle of harm toward him. I would hope that any managers of mine would treat me better than that. Moreover, as noted it also has the potential to create significant practical management problems that waste large amounts of time and energy, and reduce morale and productivity. In my opinion, it is the worst choice on all important grounds.

The main problem with the second solution, that of disregarding my boss's suggestion and addressing the problem myself, is its threat to my career. There must be some personally less threatening ways to deal with the casual suggestions of my boss and thus relieve me of their burden. Once I have done so, I am free to address the problem of Toivo in some more creative and less ethically and practically objectionable ways.

My decision would be first to have a serious, in-depth, heart-to-heart talk with my boss, explaining to him in a very diplomatic and inoffensive way all the disadvantages of shifting Toivo around. I would do so in a way making it obvious that upper management would likely look askance on that solution. I would then proceed to explain the nature of the ethically acceptable alternative measures available and outline my plan to pursue them. This would show him that I have taken his suggestions seriously, value his opinions, and am bent on addressing the problem in a way that is best for the company overall. I think that once he realizes the significance of the union-management conflict that could result from shifting Toivo around, he may well be willing to admit that we should just turn our backs on Toivo. If so, he might then suggest that I simply drop all concern with Toivo. But I think I can take steps that may have some hope of success and that would cost the company very little.

The only problem with my approach is the possibility that my boss might be bull-headed about it all and insist that I defer to his greater experience and authority. If I were to do so, I would be setting myself up for a very bad JPR in the future and would reduce my chances for advancement. However, if my boss turned out to be that autocratic, there would be no solutions that would be good for me personally. Clearly, then, my best approach is to use every means at my disposal to convince him of the benefits of my handling the case in the best way I know how.

❏ 5.3 Sin of Omission

You live in a city of about 50,000 people, and sell real estate for a local realtor. Your client, Ms. Boltuc, is single and middle-aged, and a new arrival in town. She is looking for a small house suitable for her to live in alone. You have shown her several houses in her price range, one of which appeals to her because it is attractive, well cared for, and located in a pleasant neighborhood.

Despite its appeal, the house does, to her mind, have a drawback. It is older than she had wanted, and she is concerned about buying an older home. She is afraid of hidden problems in its plumbing, electrical service, or structure that might cost her more in the next few years than she can afford.

You have a strong desire to make a sale. The market has been depressed for several months now, and you have not sold a house in more than a month. Your bills have been mounting, and there is pressure from home to "bring home the bacon."

In mulling over the problem, one thought occurs to you that might offer a solution. You could suggest to Ms. Boltuc that she call the City Hall and ask one of their housing inspectors to check out the house and give her a report. Although the city does not advertise this service, it does let its inspectors inspect houses for individuals, for a fee of $60. The unbiased opinion of an impartial third party might well allay Ms. Boltuc's worries and secure the sale.

The problem with such an approach is that the city inspectors are famous for the trivial nature of many of their observations. When you bought your own house last year and had it inspected, they turned in a long list of very petty violations of city code. They listed the lack of a hand rail in the stairway to the basement, the lack of an overhead light in a hallway and the lack of an exhaust fan in a bathroom. Although they did not require you to remedy such infractions, you are afraid that a similar list might well scare off Ms. Boltuc for false reasons.

You have no clear legal obligation to suggest that Ms. Boltuc look into this city service nor to tell her there is such a service. The National Association of Realtors Code of Ethics does not specifically state that one should inform one's clients of such a service. Article 9 of the NAR code requires realtors to avoid "exaggeration, misrepresentation, or concealment of pertinent facts relating to the property or the transaction."* But it does not require realtors to inform clients of all possible ways in which they may obtain opinions about a house. Article 9 is broadly interpreted to refer to the condition of a house itself and services that the realtor offers the client. Local realtors interpret it to refer to facts about the house rather than facts about what one may do to gather further information about a house. Indeed, it is standard practice among local realtors to *avoid* mentioning the inspection service to clients, and to sell houses that have not been inspected.

It is clear at this point that in order to sell the house, you will have to promote it strongly. You believe honestly that the house is in "good condition." But you now wonder if you have any ethical obligation to inform Ms. Boltuc about the city inspection service. What should you do? Analyze the case until it is RESOLVEDD.

☐ 5.4 An Analysis of "Sin of Omission"

This case is clearly irrelevant to the law and on the fringe of professional ethics. Ethics does play a role in the case, however, for I must consider Ms. Boltuc's well-being as well as my own. To satisfy my own needs should not be my only goal as a salesperson. In making a sale, I also have a responsibility to help my client.

The mere fact that other real estate salespersons do not inform their clients of such information does not make it right. Established practice may be a reason to do something, but should not be the only reason.

* *It's Your Association*, pamphlet of the National Association of Realtors, 1989.

In my analysis, I will need to consider very carefully the relevance of the principle of equal consideration of interests, as I do have an obligation to treat my client in a manner in which I would be willing to be treated myself.

The principal ethical issue in the case is whether or not I owe it to Ms. Boltuc to give her this information. It is the proper relationship between real estate salespeople and their clients that needs to be considered.

There are three main solutions to the case. First, I could do as my competitors do and not tell Ms. Boltuc about the city inspection service. Second, I could inform her of the service and take the accompanying risks. Third, I could have the inspection done without her knowledge and decide what to do with the information later.

If I choose the first solution and do not tell her about the service, she may or may not buy the house, and it is not clear at this point which is more likely. If I try to promote the house strongly, this might work or might scare her off. But if she finds out about the service from someone else, she may wonder why I did not tell her, and she may lose trust in me.

The only reason I would choose to withhold the information from Ms. Boltuc would be to facilitate the sale of the house. Doing so would be motivated partly by the desire to benefit myself. But since I think the house is a good buy for her, withholding the information may benefit her. So withholding would uphold egoistic value and also her well-being.

Withholding this information from Ms. Boltuc would violate the principles of autonomy and fidelity. I would be deliberately withholding information that could enhance her ability to make a more informed choice. I would be making this decision partly for egoistic reasons and partly to promote her best interests. But I would be withholding information that she could use and would be doing so without her consent. So it could be argued that withholding would be a breach of trust.

If, however, I choose the second solution and tell Ms. Boltuc about the service, she may or may not decide to use it. And it is not at all clear whether her using it would or would not have a strong influence on her decision. If I explain to her how petty much of the inspectors' reports are, this might neutralize some of her concern. My telling her might also increase her respect for and trust in me. Whether or not she buys the house, informing her could in turn lead her to recommend future clients to me.

Telling her would uphold the principles of autonomy and fidelity by enhancing her ability to make a well-informed decision and by giving her this relevant and possibly helpful information. It would not violate any important ethical values, although it might, arguably, be a sacrifice of my own egoistic value.

If I choose the third solution and order the inspection done without telling her, I may have to pay for it myself. Or I might be able to persuade the owner of the house, or even Ms. Boltuc, to pay for it. If the inspection came out well, it might be a significant selling point for Ms. Boltuc. If it did not come out well, I could drop it or decide to show it to Ms. Boltuc anyway. Several options would still be open.

Ordering the inspection without telling Ms. Boltuc might uphold my own egoistic advantage and might help Ms. Boltuc if it helped her realize what a good house it really is. It might, thus, uphold the principles of autonomy and fidelity by helping her to decide and by my doing my best for her. The fact that it might cost me some money shows I am willing to take a risk for her benefit.

Ordering the inspection on my own violates the principles of autonomy and fidelity in different ways. First, ordering the inspection is done primarily for my benefit. She would not be in a position to make any decision about the inspection report unless I decide to tell her about it. So this solution might well be motivated primarily by my own desires and only secondarily by concern for her well-being. And I would be acting faithfully to her only after I had determined that telling her would benefit me.

The third solution, ordering the inspection myself, has serious disadvantages. First, doing so places my own well-being above that of Ms. Boltuc. There would be no good reason to inform her of the inspection unless it turned out well. If it turned out poorly and I informed her I had had it done, that would simply scare her off. Second, if I told her about the inspection after it was done she might wonder why I had not told her first. She might think that I was simply pulling strings behind her back and might lose trust in me. This solution would violate the principles of autonomy and fidelity and risk my reputation. It is best avoided.

Evaluation of the outcomes and likely impact of the first two solutions provides little help in resolving the case. The consequences of neither decision are more likely to occur than those of the other. The ethical values at stake in the case are somewhat more helpful, for the failure to inform Ms. Boltuc would violate the principles of autonomy and fidelity. However, I do not think that either principle is seriously violated by withholding the information. Salespeople are not expected to inform their clients of every possible avenue they might pursue to arrive at a decision. Both the lack of clarity on the matter in the National Association of Realtors' Code of Ethics and the standard practice of other salespeople support this point. Moreover, the city does not advertise the presence of the service and seems unconcerned to encourage people to use it.

The facts that I very much need to make a sale and Ms. Boltuc needs a house are important aspects of this case. My own desire to make the sale, together with my knowledge of her needs, incline me to be extremely positive about the house. But this worries me. I might be too positive and apply too much pressure and thereby scare her off. I need to be aware of the limitations of my own ability to influence her, and the possibility that the "hard sell" might backfire. The point here is that even my own egoistic needs do not clearly show that withholding the information is the most effective way to make the sale or to benefit myself or her.

On balance, then, only two considerations reveal a significant difference between the two best choices of telling or not telling: the principles of autonomy and fidelity. Withholding the information is a violation (even if only a weak one) of these ethical principles, and telling her about the inspection service is not. These two principles are the single outstanding considerations in the case, and convince me that I should indeed tell her about the city inspection service.

I would tell her about the service and explain to her carefully the nature of the report that would result. In doing so, I would not try to scare her, but would simply try to be straightforward, working toward the single goal of helping her as best I can. That way, she can decide for herself whether she wants to use the service. And if she makes the decision herself, she is less likely to be shocked by the results of the inspection.

My decision to tell her does have a number of advantages. First of all, my telling her is more clearly ethical than not telling her. Furthermore, in doing so, there are advantages for me personally. For one thing, I will have no doubts that I am doing my best for her. For another, this can only help my reputation in the long run. Finally, even if she does not choose to buy the house, she may come to trust me and develop a sense of loyalty to me and ask me to show her other houses. I may end up selling her a house after all, even if not this one.

The only serious disadvantage of this decision is the possibility that she may, as a result, buy neither this house nor another one from me. But the disadvantage of this decision does not point to a corresponding advantage of the alternate decisions. There is no good reason to think that withholding the information or ordering the inspection myself would be any more likely to secure the sale.

□ □ □ □ □ □ □

Cases: Personal Ethical Conflicts for Analysis

□ I. Too Personal to Ask

VIOLATIONS OF PRIVACY IN HIRING AND TESTING

For three years you had worked in the personnel office of Jefferson Security, a private security company that provided security guards for banks, malls, and other businesses. Your job was to interview prospective employees and administer the company's personality exam, a standard requirement in the security field. The candidates that you interviewed had all been carefully screened for criminal records and had placed well on the aptitude tests given to every promising applicant. Your job was to judge their character through a personal interview and administer the personality exam.

Until this week you had enjoyed the job and felt confident that between the interview and the test, you were giving objective evaluations of the candidates' honesty and trustworthiness. But now there was a problem brought about by the institution of a new personality exam. Your supervisor had instructed you to use the new, "more accurate and in-depth" exam and to do away with the old, "rather cold and impersonal" one. You decided to review the new exam to see how much improvement had been made in the questions.

As you began reading the questions, your anticipation turned to disbelief. Some questions seemed overly personal, while others could not possibly be answered without reflecting poorly on anyone who replied honestly. Scanning the question booklet, you saw the following true-false questions:

Sexual things disgust me.

As a child, there were times I hated my parents.

I feel like jumping off when I'm on a high place.

I have never done anything I was punished for.

I have never had black, tarry bowel movements.

There is nothing wrong with masturbating.

There is a big difference between a person who steals because he has to and a person who steals because he wants to.

I often insist on doing things my own way.

Low wages force employees to steal from their employers.

I have never taken anything home from places where I have worked in the past.

Some of the other questions required short essays, and included questions very much like the true-false ones. No honest person could complete this test without looking like a thief or a liar.

As you sat and considered what to do, you remembered reading about a lawsuit brought against a company that had used just such a test. A famous Yale law professor had taken the case to court. The article included an interview in which the professor had said that such tests were seriously flawed. The answers were supposed to help employers predict future dishonest actions, but when used as criteria for hiring they could cause a person to be denied a job without ever having done anything wrong. They were, she had said, potentially discriminatory, an unconstitutional invasion of privacy, and contained questions that were unrelated to the job or its requirements. Your new test seemed to have all those flaws and more.

You decided to talk to your supervisor. After listening to your reservations about the test, he tried to explain the theory behind the test. He said that a security job demands employees of the highest moral character and that the test is designed to evaluate a person's character. Then he enumerated three factors involved in employee dishonesty: opportunity, attitude, and need. Opportunities will always be there, and needs may arise any time in the future. But if the employee has the right attitude, he is unlikely to act dishonestly. If an employee has the attitude that dishonesty or theft is OK, then any unimportant need may trigger him to break the law. Moreover, since other security companies began using the test, the number of complaints against their guards had declined dramatically.

It sounds good in theory, you thought. But what about all those problems mentioned by the law professor? What about the invasion of an applicant's privacy? Or the fact that almost any honest person has to look bad when answering these questions truthfully? Does any employer have a right to this kind of compromising information about anyone? It would be difficult to give your own mother such information, let alone some stranger in a personnel office. And how do questions about your bowel movements, sexuality, and masturbation help predict whether you will act dishonestly?

Noting that you are bothered about administering the test, the personnel director suggested that you take the day to think it over, and return tomorrow. If you felt you could not administer the test to people, he would see about giving you another assignment or transferring you elsewhere. He assured you that none of this would be held against you and that he was sure you would come to the right conclusion.

Should you administer the test or not? You wonder whether the company will hold it against you if you refuse to use the test. Besides, you genuinely enjoy doing the interviews and can't think of another job that you'd want in the company. But you are very troubled by the kinds of questions asked and the issue of privacy they raised. By tomorrow, however, the problem must be RESOLVEDD, because a room full of applicants will be waiting for you at 9 A.M.

☐ 2. It's Not My Union

CROSSING A PICKET LINE

The strike at Carbon Manufacturing Company had been going on for about four weeks when you saw the ad in the paper that read, "Jobs, jobs, jobs! Carbon Manufacturing is looking for employees in all departments. High pay, benefits, no union dues. Apply at the personnel department."

Knowing that the Carbon plant was a union shop and that the strike was under way, you figured this was a temporary position with no future. Then a friend informed you that he had applied and was told that the company planned to replace the union strikers permanently. He explained that the pay was at current union levels and benefits were pretty good. The only catch was that the company expected you never to join a union.

Because you needed a job, this all sounded very interesting. However, you were bothered by the prospect of being a scab, and also by the nonunion clause. Your father had been a strong union man and had taught you about the good that unions had done for working Americans. Before unions existed, the pay was low, hours long, benefits few, and there was no job security.

Such poor working conditions, you believe, are a thing of the past, and it did not seem to you that there was still a need for unions. In fact, they seem outdated and, because of their constant unreasonable demands on management, partly to blame for our falling behind countries like Japan, where unions do not exist or have little influence. So, lacking your father's strong commitment to unionism, you are seriously tempted to apply for a job at Carbon Manufacturing.

Yet you do recognize that the local union has done good things for your neighbors, and that you are a part of the community that has benefited from the union's activities. Indeed, many of your family and friends are members of the union. Moreover, if you sign up as a scab, you could find yourself in the middle of some violence when crossing the picket lines. Should you apply for the job and thus undermine the union?

Your problem stems in part from the fact that you have had nothing but low-paying jobs in local burger joints and grocery stores for the last six months. Your employment problem arose after the closing of the plant where you worked as a maintenance mechanic. You are trained to fix many different kinds of machines, from lathes to punch presses and more, and genuinely resent having to sling burgers or pack bags of groceries. Lately your self-esteem has dropped in direct proportion to your time out of work. Your wife and two children have been very understanding, but you feel as though you are not doing as well for them as you were when you brought home a larger paycheck. The job you are eligible for at Carbon would pay almost as much as you were getting after three years in your previous position.

Although you have not yet made up your mind, you visit Carbon's personnel office, where your interview goes well and you are offered a job. The personnel manager explains that if the strike is settled, you will be kept on in the same position, regardless of whether the union workers return. However, the job does require that you sign a statement agreeing not to join a union as long as you are employed at Carbon.

Where do your loyalties lie? What are your priorities and obligations? Make the decision, analyzing the issues until they are RESOLVEDD.

❑ 3. Is This Nutritional?

CAN YOU WORK FOR A TOBACCO COMPANY?

Lately, you have been thinking about searching for a new job. The company you work for, Nutritional Products, Inc., was recently bought by a large conglomerate, ABC Industries, whose major source of income (72 percent of their sales) comes from the sale of tobacco products, primarily cigarettes. Although your job and tasks have not changed since the merger, you are bothered by what you take to be a conflict of interest between your role as a nutritional researcher and the parent company's sale of cigarettes.

"How can I consider myself a health care professional and work for a company that sells a product that is known to be dangerous to the health of millions of people?" you ask Todd, your associate.

"You don't have anything to do with those sales. Why worry about it?" he replies.

"I know the dangers," you continue, "and am opposed to people smoking. We have a no-smoking policy in the labs. My whole job and life's work are directed to promoting good health. Drawing a paycheck from a tobacco company seems hypocritical."

"Look, the parent company has nothing to do with the running of the daily operation here. In fact, they've left us alone and allowed us to continue just as we always have. They haven't even mentioned the negative report on tobacco products that one of the labs is doing. Clearly, they look at us just as an investment. So long as we're profitable, there's no interference."

"True, but Todd, I feel guilty about it. I can't tell you how upset I was when my grandfather died of lung cancer from smoking for fifty years. Now I'm working for a company that's selling what killed him."

"Hey, no offense, but wasn't it his choice to smoke? No one forced him. If he kept smoking after the Surgeon General's report and all the negative publicity, I'd say it was his choice and he decided to take the risk. And besides, doesn't the company say that the Surgeon General's report is not 100 percent proof that smoking leads to lung cancer?"

"Well, maybe, but nicotine is addictive—"

"Oh, wait a minute! 'Addictive' is a loaded term. If I eat five chocolate bars a day, or drink 10 colas, no one says I'm addicted. I can quit whenever I want. If smoking were addictive, how come so many people have just quit? It's a free choice. Seems to me that 'addiction' is used for someone else's habit that we disapprove of. Anyway, smoking is legal, selling cigarettes is legal, and the work you're doing here does help people, so you're not doing anything to hurt people personally. Why not just look at it that way?"

"I don't know. It bothers me," you respond.

"Enough to quit? Enough to leave in the middle of your research project? No one else here can finish that project as well as you. I think you owe some loyalty to us, too."

"I'm not sure I can look at it that way. People die from smoking, that's the bottom line."

This is a decision calling for careful reflection and evaluation of the relevant values. What is the best thing for you to do? Analyze the case until it is RESOLVEDD.

☐ 4. "But I Need This Job . . . And That One"
LOOKING FOR A NEW JOB ON COMPANY TIME

You have been working for Rocky Road Insurance Agency for over five years. In that time you worked your way up from a summer intern to a claims adjuster before becoming an assistant account executive. Your basic duties include a good deal of phone work, customer relations, and re-evaluation of customers' policies to fit their changing needs. In the six months that you have been in this new position, you have been praised for your ability to handle customer needs quickly, efficiently, and courteously. A number of major clients have even mentioned your abilities to the head of the agency.

Rocky Road is a small, private, family-owned, independent insurance agency that handles accounts for a number of different insurance companies. The agency was started and is still run by James Witucki, the president and sole owner. It has grown from its original staff of nineteen to a staff of eighty-five, and Witucki is contemplating expansion into other cities. Yet Witucki is hesitant to expand too much, as he feels this will compromise the company's strengths: personal, fast, and efficient customer service. He is aware of your abilities and considers you a potential senior executive.

However, you have received job offers from other agencies that have heard of your abilities. Some customers have asked if you would be interested in joining them as vice president of your own insurance division. So far you have politely turned them down, feeling a certain loyalty to Rocky Road and to Jim Witucki, who hired you as an undergraduate trainee, trained you, and promoted you steadily to your present position.

Lately, your wife and father have been telling you that you are being overly loyal and may be sacrificing greater job opportunities than are available at Rocky Road. At a larger company, they believe, you could make a third more money and probably advance to the level of senior vice president or CEO, both of which you can't do at Rocky Road because Jim and his family occupy all those positions.

As a result of the offers and your family's pressure, you have been checking into the proposals made to you, as well as making inquiries at other agencies and corporations. The results have been positive. In fact, you now have four interviews scheduled at different agencies in the next two weeks. During lunch with Martha Bower, another employee who worked her way from summer intern (she was hired at the same time as you) to management, you tell her about the interviews.

"How can you get to these interviews?" she asks, "Who will cover for you while you're gone?"

"What do you mean, 'cover for me'? I'll get the messages the next day when I come back to work. I'll handle them then."

"What? And compromise your reputation as 'Mr Efficiency'? But seriously, have you told Jim about the situation? There are lots of things that come in on the phone that you should handle immediately. What will he say if no one is there to handle them?"

"No, I haven't told Jim. I'm afraid to. He started me off in the business and has always been good to me. I don't want to hurt his feelings or make him mad at me. After all, I may not take any of these jobs, and I'd like a place to come back to."

Martha pauses for a moment, then says, "You don't want to hurt his feelings, but you're willing to let your job slide while you explore other opportunities at competing firms? What are you going to do, call in sick on the days you have interviews?"

"Actually, I don't have any sick days coming, so I thought I'd work half-days and just leave early like I do when I have to meet with clients. Nobody ever asks or seems to care when I go out early. I guess they just figure I'm working. What's the big deal, anyway? Everyone does this now and then. It's one of the benefits of being in management. Any emergencies will wait for twenty-four hours, won't they? It's not like I'm a paramedic, you know."

"Boy, I sure wouldn't do it that way. It seems, you know, sort of sneaky. Doesn't Jim have the right to know? Maybe he can match the offers. Besides, don't you owe him some loyalty, given that he hired and trained you? Suppose there's some emergency when you're out and no one is here to answer a client's call? Won't that look bad for you and the company even if it can wait until the next day? Come on, Jim deserves better than that."

"Whoa, what about me? I busted a gut the last five years. Jim's gotten his money's worth from me. Everybody job-hunts on company time, anyway. I mean, I'll tell him in plenty of time if I decide to leave. I'll even train my replacement, if he wants me to. Don't I have a right to do what's best for me?"

"Well, those are nice ideas! I thought better of you. You're going to ignore your job here while interviewing elsewhere, compromise the firm's reputation if anything goes wrong, skip out on Jim without much of a warning, and who knows what else! I thought you believed in loyalty and gratitude, but I guess you're interested in your own skin first, just like everyone else." Martha stood up and left in disgust.

What should you do? Consider the alternatives, the pros and cons of each, analyze the case until it is RESOLVEDD, and make a decision.

☐ 5. So, What Are the Standards?

HIDDEN PROMOTION REQUIREMENTS AND WHISTLEBLOWING

You work for Utopia Manufacturing, a medium-size company employing about 375 people, with sales around $35 million annually. Utopia produces various sorts of electrical supplies for the construction industry. Utopia prides itself on its fairness and generosity toward its employees. Until now, you had thought this pride was well justified. However, you now have doubts about Utopia's claim of fairness and openness. You have discovered that Utopia's stated policy for determining wage increases seems very different from the actual practices. The stated policy is objective and open, but the actual practices make use of unstated and supposedly prohibited standards.

You are presently employed at Utopia as a skilled blue-collar worker in the machine shop, where you have worked for eight years. Following Utopia's creation of a student aid co-op program, you returned to school to finish your bachelor's degree in business, which you had begun many years ago before dropping out. Later you completed Utopia's machinist training program. Utopia is now paying your way toward your master's degree in business administration and wants to employ you in a middle-level management position once you complete your degree.

One class you were required to take was business ethics. During the course, you decided to write a paper on Utopia's wage evaluation policy as an example of a fair, honest, and ethical business practice. While you were researching this paper, your views about fairness at Utopia crumbled.

You had decided to analyze Utopia's guidelines for raises in Area Six, the area where you work. Three friends of yours in management agreed to help your research. You began by interviewing Danny Rose, Area Six day shift supervisor, who was personally responsible for initiating pay raises there. During your taped interview, Danny said, "The most important thing I look for is attitude and initiative. If an employee has those two, then I will probably grant a raise. I evaluate progress and potential, as well as productivity. If an employee's attitude and initiative are good though there may be problems in other areas, I wouldn't hold the employee back."

You also interviewed Celia Weinstein, plant superintendent and former Area Six supervisor. She said, "The supervisor really knows how capable employees are. Unless I have specific knowledge to indicate that the supervisor's opinion is wrong, I approve wage increases. I don't have detailed enough information on any one employee to do a complete evaluation. But I do look for employee dependability. If I know I can count on someone's willingness to be called to work twenty-four hours a day, that's who will get the raise."

Jamaal Rashid, director of human resources, works with upper management, especially the vice president of production, to determine guidelines for hiring, firing, promotions, and raises. He showed you the employee review sheet that he developed with other managers during a brainstorming session and that is used to determine all wage increases. But Jamaal pointed out that no two people are the same. Although the sheet lists only objective factors, he looks for a good attitude and desire to work as the two most important elements in determining raises. Thus, you have concluded that the three people most directly involved in the wage increase process use initiative, attitude, willingness to work, and dependability as the key factors in granting raises.

Although all this sounds fine, the problem arises from the content of the policy guidelines themselves. Listed on the evaluation sheet are

(1) time of service, (2) production rate, (3) quality of production, (4) knowledge of production methods, and (5) continued training. Each factor is to be rated on a scale of 1 to 10. Each of the five, moreover, is fairly easy to judge, since each involves easily quantifiable and objective factors. Nowhere on the sheet did you find the subjective factors of attitude, initiative, willingness to work, or dependability, none of which can be clearly determined on the basis of observation. However, your main worry is that these standards are all unstated. Moreover, the union contract for Area Six employees states that such subjective considerations are *not* to be taken into account when considering wage increases.

Aided further by other friends in the office, you uncovered a confidential memo from the vice president of production to all evaluators. The memo explicitly approves the *unstated* standards and emphasizes that they should be the most important factors in determining raises or promotions. But the policy statement given to the union and distributed to all employees clearly states that to move from Pay Rate 4 up to Rate 3 all that is required is four years of experience. To move from Rate 3 to Rate 2, one must have, in addition to six years of experience, a job proficiency rating of 8 or higher. To move from Rate 2 to Rate 1 requires, besides seven years of experience and a proficiency rating of 8, a rating of 8 or higher in job knowledge, and evidence of continued training. None of the subjective factors were mentioned.

It became clear to you by the time you finished this research that the company uses a completely hidden set of standards, misleads the union and workers, and does so with the approval of all the managers involved in the evaluation process. There is no question that this practice is entirely unethical.

The question, however, is what you should do about it. You have taped interviews and a confidential memo as evidence. The memo was obtained secretly, the interviews given by people you went to as friends and who trust you, while the whole project was a result of Utopia's willingness to help pay for your schooling to advance your career. All the blue-collar workers have been systematically lied to, and are being evaluated using hidden standards to which they cannot object nor reply should their raises be denied.

To whom do you owe your allegiance? How can you take steps to correct the situation without betraying the trust or jeopardizing the jobs of those who helped you? What, moreover, would be the best steps for the company to take? How could you proceed without losing your job and the education Utopia is providing you? Analyze the situation until it is RESOLVEDD.

☐ 6. Deception or Shrewd Bargaining?
WHAT CONSTITUTES UNFAIR CONTRACT NEGOTIATING?

Having been a legal secretary for nearly nine years, you are familiar with many of the provisions of the American Bar Association's code of ethics and various definitions of what is considered fair bargaining in negotiations. Specifically, you know that no material facts should be withheld by either side in negotiating salaries and payments for services. Rule 4.1 of the ABA Model Rules states, "Under generally accepted conventions in negotiation, certain types of statements ordinarily are not taken as statements of material fact. Estimates of price or value placed on the subject of transaction and a party's intention as to an acceptable settlement of a claim are in this category."* You looked this up because you were bothered by the present course of your negotiations with your boss regarding your salary and bonuses for the new fiscal year. In particular, you wondered if it was really fair for you to tell him that you would not accept anything less than an 8 percent raise and a bonus of $1,000 (10 percent more than your previous bonus), although in fact you know that you would be quite happy to get a 4 percent raise and the same bonus.

Is it a "material fact" that you are in reality willing to accept much less than what you told him last week? According to your grasp of the law, a material fact is one that, if known to the ignorant party, would reasonably be expected to cause that party to behave differently. It seems to you that if your boss knew you'd settle for less than you said, he would negotiate differently with you and with the other partners in the law firm who must approve all raises and bonuses. Legally, fraud is involved if one party has "superior knowledge." Superior knowledge is the grasp of material facts that the other party lacks, and that the other party, if not told, would be unlikely to discover. "Surely," you think, "I am in that position when it comes to knowing that I'll settle for less. My boss can't possibly get inside my head to find this out."

To double-check, you asked Vera Browning, an associate in the

* American Bar Association Model Rules of Professional Conduct, *Selected Statutes, Rules, and Standards on the Legal Profession* (St. Paul, MN: West, 1987).

firm and a close personal friend of yours, what she thought about all this. She acknowledged that the ABA's code seems to exclude your intentions as material facts. However, she pointed out that according to common law "If one party to a contract . . . has superior knowledge that is not within the fair and reasonable reach of the other party and which the second could not discover by the exercise of reasonable diligence, or (if the first party has) means of knowledge that are not open to both parties alike, he [the first party] is under a legal obligation to speak."*

Then she added, "But look, we women have been too easy in negotiating here. These senior partners have been taking advantage of us because we are too polite, too timid to play the game the way they do. So my advice is that, where the law seems ambiguous, go for it—play it tough. Bluff and negotiate hard. You don't owe them a peek into your head. Would they give you one into theirs?"

All in all, you are bothered by the conflicting ethics and legality of your negotiations. But isn't this all just part of shrewd bargaining? Surely any good salesperson keeps this kind of information under the table when he or she haggles over prices? When you bought your house, the real estate salesman quoted a price that was higher than the seller was willing to accept. You didn't see any ethical or legal problem there. In fact, when you sold some property last year, you had the same salesman handle the account because of his shrewd sales techniques.

In addition, you feel sure that your boss's initial offer is less than he is willing to pay you. So aren't you both just playing the same game? Where does shrewd, but ethical, negotiating end and fraud or unethical deception begin? According to what you know about the ABA's guidelines and legal definitions, this *could* be unethical or even fraudulent negotiating. Yet, as Vera said, the whole question of what is legal is unclear. Besides, you are sure you're worth the money you asked for, and you are sure your boss thinks so, too. But then again, he's not just a stranger: you've worked with him for seven years and gotten to know him quite well. So don't you owe it to him to be honest? Hasn't that been the key to your successful working relationship? The question that nags you now is whether he has been honest with you.

Tomorrow you have a crucial meeting with him to hammer out the final details of the raise and bonus proposal he will take to the next

* American Jurisprudence 2d, Vol. 37: *Fraud and Deceit* (San Francisco: Lawyers Cooperative Publishing, 1968), section 148.

partners' meeting. What should you tell him? What offer should you make? You want to be fair and ethical, but also want to avoid being the pushover Vera hinted you would be if you didn't stick to your first ultimatum. The problem needs to be RESOLVEDD before the meeting at 9 A.M. tomorrow.

❑ 7. The Price of Honesty
USING YOUR POSITION TO DUMP AN UNPLEASANT EMPLOYEE

You are the personnel manager for a manufacturing company employing 110 workers. You have held the position for two years and, except for one problem, have enjoyed the job. That problem is a worker, Davis Meany, nicknamed the Lawyer, who falls into the category you like to call the "if only" group, meaning "If only there were some way to get rid of this guy, I'd do it in a minute."

The Lawyer has been with the company for almost ten years, works as a warehouse clerk, and is protected by a strong union contract. He has an annoying mastery of the details of that contract. Whenever he's given an order he doesn't like, he cites some clause in the contract that gives him a way out. Often he is right, although careful scrutiny would reveal that some of his claims are misreadings of the contract. Rarely does anyone challenge him, however, because of his nasty temper and the fact that it is usually easier to assign the task to someone else.

Meany's attitude and the fact that he stands up to the bosses with impunity has lowered morale among the other warehouse employees. They think they are being forced to work harder to cover for him. Yet whenever management has tried to correct the problem, the other union workers unite firmly behind the Lawyer and assert his rights "under the terms of the contract." You suspect they are afraid that if the company forces Meany to follow orders, they will all lose some of their guaranteed protections. So they seem willing to put up with all the problems rather than compromise the contract.

Recently, Meany has been coming to work late, leaving for long washroom breaks, and sometimes going home early. The terms of the contract do not allow you to cut his pay unless he misses more than a half hour a day, which he never does. This "five minutes here, ten minutes there" practice has also affected the attitudes of some workers, even outside of the warehouse. They seem to admire his nerve in standing up to you and the bosses, and their work habits seemed to have slipped a bit, too. Other workers seem to resent his practices. But since no one will file a grievance, you can't do anything other than talk to him about his behavior.

Your attempts to counsel him and help improve his work habits have largely failed. Predictably, he has answered, "Show me the exact clause in the contract that says you can discipline me," or "Where does it say that I have to see a shrink about coming in late once in a while?" You have often felt humiliated by such discussions and spend a lot of time after each confrontation thinking, "If only there were a way—"

The plant manager, following your last discussion about the problem, shouted, "GET RID OF THIS GUY, I DON'T CARE HOW. I DON'T EVEN WANT TO KNOW."

Later that week, you received a phone call that presented a tempting opportunity. Sajid Singh, the personnel manager from a comparably sized company, located in the same town, and with which you do a small amount of business, wanted some information about a prospective employee. He told you that one of the clerks from your company has applied for a job as the warehouse supervisor at his plant. Singh asks if you or your company would mind if he offered this clerk a job that included a raise and promotion. He is concerned that you not feel that they had "stolen one of your best workers." You are overjoyed when you learn that the clerk in question is none other than Davis Meany, the Lawyer! You respond by saying, "We would never stand in the way of one of our employees leaving for greener pastures."

Singh says he appreciates your understanding and hopes you can help him with one final detail. He says that his company has no doubts about the man's capabilities, since he's been working in various warehouse positions for close to twenty years. He has shown that he's a steady and trustworthy worker employed by your company for almost ten years. Moreover, he claims that your company has never had a single complaint about him. However, they need a strong letter of recommendation to back up their hiring him because two other qualified candidates are still in the running, although they're the second and third choices behind Meany.

"What I need," Singh says, "is an honest evaluation of his capabilities, attitudes, and work habits to go along with his excellent résumé and successful interview." Once he receives the letter, which is really a technicality, Singh tells you, they'll be making the man "an offer he can't refuse."

Having told Singh you would get to work immediately checking out all the details and talking to everyone who would have knowledge of Meany's performance, you hang up the phone and lean back in your chair, thinking, " 'If only' time is here!" Then you wonder, "Can it really be this easy? Should I really do this?" Well, should you? If they're so impressed with him and believe his representations of himself, isn't that their problem? Analyze the case until it is RESOLVEDD.

❑ 8. It's Your Choice
FORCING EMPLOYEES TO LEAVE A COMPANY

You are a midlevel manager working for a giant multinational corporation that has been going through some rough economic times. Out of a total worldwide work force of 350,000, the company has lost 34,000 employees during the past five years. The company's annual earnings estimate has fallen to below $7 a share, from last year's $10.45 a share, on earnings of $6.02 billion. New estimates for the second-quarter earnings are now below $1 a share, compared to last year's $2.45, or $1.41 billion. This continues a trend begun almost five years earlier.

During the tough economic period, the company set up a voluntary program that gave incentives to employees who sought work at other companies. This was done in order to honor a "no firings" pledge the company had upheld ever since its founding decades before. The voluntary programs included incentives for early retirement, quitting, and expenses incurred if an employee took a job with another noncompetitive company.

Upper management now believes there is a problem with the voluntary programs. It seems that too many of the company's good workers have taken advantage of the incentives, while many weaker employees remain. An internal study done by the company's industrial psychology department concludes that productivity is down 20 percent among remaining workers, mainly due to the fact that many of the best employees have left the company.

The accounting department has recommended reducing the work force by another 14,000 in order to reduce further profit loss. This has created a problem for the company: how to cut the work force while honoring the "no firing" pledge and still hang on to the best workers.

On your desk is a memo from the highest level stating that a new policy is in effect. The memo outlines a program that allows managers to "encourage" certain targeted employees to leave the company. The memo also notes that many of the weaker employees have been laid off indefinitely, thereby technically adhering to the no-firing policy. However, certain targeted employees cannot be laid off, because of the terms of their contracts. You are being told to "encourage" these employees to leave. Attached to the memo is a list of four expendable employees who work in your department. The list ends with the statement "You are to convince said employees that seeking employment elsewhere would be to their best interest."

Through the managers' grapevine, you learn that a dim view will be taken of middle managers who cannot "encourage" the targeted employees to move on. As you contemplate the memo and the pressure being put on you and the other managers, it strikes you that at least two employees named on your list are people whose work you have always considered to be well above average. And not on the list are two people whose work you believe is marginal. No guidelines or reasons are given explaining how the company decided who would be put on the list and who would not.

The whole situation has you deeply troubled. You think that this is a violation of the spirit of the no-firing policy. Yet you are aware that the best hope for the company's continued economic survival is to cut back its work force. You are also bothered by the two people on the list who do not deserve to be eliminated and who have considerable value to the company. Finally, you have no real idea of how to go about "encouraging" people to leave jobs they have held, in all four cases, for at least five years.

After speaking to the head of personnel about the policy and your questions, you are still unsure of how to proceed. She has told you that it is really up to you how to convince the employees to leave. Furthermore, if you feel that some of the people on your list are there by mistake, you must prepare a memo outlining your objections and suggesting alternate names that might replace them on the list.

She also notes that those employees who leave will be given two weeks' severance pay for every year they've worked at the company. But this offer is good only for those who leave voluntarily before the end of the next month. After that, there will be no severance pay for employees who leave voluntarily or who are fired. Your job is to inform marginal employees who want to stay that their pay may be cut or that they may be fired eventually.

It seems clear to you that the company is not simply encouraging voluntary participation. Rather, it is pressuring certain employees into quitting. The token adherence to the no-firing policy seems to be a mere sham. But if you fail to carry out company orders, you yourself may well be considered marginal.

There are a number of options. You may adhere to the list, refuse to do the company's dirty work, or come up with some better way of handling your situation. Which is best, and for what reasons? Analyze the case until it is RESOLVEDD.

☐ 9. A Spy in the House
THE LEAKING OF TRADE SECRETS

Returning from a meeting of Galesburg Data Corporation's area supervisors, you can't stop wondering about the people you thought you knew and could trust. You worry about the six people in your own research group. "Someone is leaking new product information to our competitor. It's got to be one of them, because it sure isn't me," you think as you pull up your chair and sit down to look over the personnel files of the six people who work for you.

After reviewing the files for about thirty minutes, you are narrowing in on Marcia Poston. There it is, staring you in the face: Marcia's husband, Tony, works for PLUSDATA, not exactly a rival company but one that previously developed some products related to your group's research. Tony Poston is listed as a data systems specialist at PLUSDATA. At the meeting PLUSDATA was discussed in detail, since it is publicizing a new data retrieval system that is almost a clone of the one your research group is working on.

But Marcia has been working with you for eleven years—eight before she married Tony. She always seemed the most trustworthy person in the group, and you can hardly imagine her telling Tony any of your company's trade secrets.

Perhaps it is someone else in the group, a disgruntled employee like Zeke Lesser, who had been turned down for promotion and had been searching for a job before deciding to stick it out at Galesburg. Had he interviewed at PLUSDATA? You don't know. You wonder, "Should I ask Zeke where he interviewed? Do I have the right to know? What if he tells me to bug off? But what if he says he *did* interview there? Can I conclude from just this that he's selling us out?" You just aren't sure what to do. It doesn't seem likely Zeke would be that sneaky or that upset about his job. But it also doesn't seem possible that Marcia could be giving away the information PLUSDATA must have used to develop its system. Nobody else in the group is really a possibility since no one else has access to the right kind of information.

You wonder how you can handle this so you don't insult anyone, create a climate of distrust, or give away your suspicions. You decide to call everyone, one by one, into your office over the next few days, explain the situation, and see what you can pick up on the matter. Perhaps you will detect some telltale signs of uneasiness in Marcia or Zeke.

During your interview with Zeke, you decide he's in the clear. He points out that he had never interviewed with PLUSDATA because he'd had a bad experience with its managers during an interview years before. "A bunch of SOB's! Only an idiot would work there," are his exact words. You wonder if he knows about Marcia's husband working there, but just chuckle to yourself and let it pass. But this does seem to leave Marcia as the only likely source of the leak.

The next day you meet with Marcia. After explaining the problem, you ask, "Is there any possibility that you know who could be leaking the information?" She answers that she has no idea at all.

"Doesn't your husband work for PLUSDATA? What exactly does he do there?" you ask.

"Yes, he works there as a data systems analyst, but you don't think I'd tell him anything about the details of our work here, do you? Sure, I complain about this or that and tell him whether the work is going well or not, but no technical details."

"Could he be putting two and two together and figuring out what we're doing here?"

"Look, Tony's not like that, he'd never do things that way! Look somewhere else. I don't like the insinuation that I'm leaking information or he's spying on us. What do you figure, he's some sort of secret agent who married me to pry out our trade secrets?"

After apologizing for being too blunt, you explain that this is the only explanation that makes sense, and that you never thought Marcia was leaking secrets or doing anything deliberately wrong. But if Marcia and Tony talk about work at home, couldn't Tony remember a good idea, forget where it came from, and think it was his own idea? "Maybe you'd better just not talk about work at all," you suggest.

Marcia says angrily, "That's crossing the line. You can't tell me what to talk to my husband about at home! We relax by talking about our days. If we couldn't do that, we'd go nuts with all this secrecy to worry about. We think of each other as one person, parts of the same whole, and I'm not going to stop talking about my problems with Tony. I don't tell him anything technical about our work. And he does not try to figure out what I'm doing. Zip, zero, end of discussion! If you bring it up again, I'll quit and really take my trade secrets with me. There's no law against that, is there?"

Now what are your options? What should you do to RESOLVE the situation at hand?

☐ 10. Spying the Spies

DO YOU REPORT A CO-WORKER'S PERSONAL DISCUSSIONS?

You worked at Galesburg Data for almost six years without anything like this happening. It struck you as very odd. Your supervisor talked to four other workers from your area in the last two days, all very "Hush, hush." The supervisor had never called you in for a "heart-to-heart talk" before, but today that changed.

As you left your supervisor's office, you wondered why she had asked you whether you discuss work-related problems with anyone. What was going on? Why did she ask you about your knowledge of what the other people in your area were working on? The supervisor had never raised such questions before. And then she rambled on about company loyalty for almost ten minutes. It just seemed weird.

Sitting at your desk near the supervisor's office, you kept thinking about events during the past month or so. It was pretty obvious something was going wrong. Then all those interviews and questions. Company loyalty? Was someone quitting, taking their knowledge of trade secrets with them?

That's it! That's what it's all about—the new project, PLUSDATA's newly announced retrieval system. It all fit. Someone had leaked information.

Just as you reached that conclusion, you saw Marcia Poston going into the supervisor's office. Something clicked. You recalled a lunch you had with Marcia and her husband about three months ago. At the time, Marcia had gone on and on about the developments in her work on Galesburg's new retrieval system. She kept asking you about your role in the project, too. You recalled nothing out of the ordinary, just the usual "shop talk." But her husband, Tony, was there, and you now realize that she had told you he worked for PLUSDATA!

Other conversations ran through your mind, and you remember at least three other times that Marcia talked about confidential information in front of her husband. None of it was anything more than harmless talk between co-workers, and she probably wasn't even aware of doing it. But there was no denying that Tony was there and probably heard more than he should have. Did Marcia talk to Tony about work-related things when they were alone? How much detail may she have given him? You can't imagine her "selling out" Galesburg. And Tony does not seem like the kind of guy who would be trying to steal trade secrets from his own wife. But it still seems to fit.

Should you tell the supervisor about your suspicions? Is there enough evidence? All you have are impressions and unreliable memories about casual conversations. Suppose you're wrong about what's going on? Suppose you're right about the problem but wrong about Marcia? Won't this hurt her both professionally and personally? How much do you owe Galesburg or your supervisor? How much do you owe Marcia, your colleague and friend? Perhaps it's best to let the supervisor do the digging and to stay out of it altogether. You are just not sure. To make a decision, you should analyze the issue until RESOLVEDD.

☐ 11. A Martini for Rossi
ALCOHOL ON THE JOB AND WHISTLEBLOWING

Edgar Rossi could have had no way of knowing that you were looking for him nor that the reassembly of an important piece of machinery for the production line was being delayed by his absence. The boss did not know that Rossi had not returned from lunch, because the boss was in a production meeting that had started during your lunch hour. But you had noticed Rossi's absence about fifteen minutes after your lunch was over.

You had just finished working on the roller bearings of the plastic molding machine. Rossi was supposed to help you on the next step when you realized that he wasn't back. This was the last step in the repair, and the other shop workers had moved temporarily to other jobs in the plant. As a result, there was no one available to ask about where Rossi was. In addition, there was no one present to fill in for

Rossi, and you weren't able to do the complicated rewiring that was his specialty.

At this point, your only choice was to search the plant for him. After looking for about twenty minutes, you bumped into Jane Howard, a good friend of Rossi's. "Have you seen Ed lately, Jane?"

"Not since lunch. I left early, but Ed stayed over at Gillard's with a friend he met there, a guy he hadn't seen for five years, who just walked in as we were leaving."

You decided that you had to check out Gillard's, a local bar and grill that is a popular lunch spot with the plant workers. You trotted down the block, entered Gillard's, and found Rossi sitting at the bar with another man.

"Rossi, come on, we've got work to do—now," you said, after exchanging greetings with both men.

"Oh, Geez, is it that late?" Rossi answered, with his words slightly slurred and the smell of liquor on his breath.

"Yeah, but Mr. Locus isn't back from his meeting yet, so he hasn't noticed you were gone."

You both ran back to the shop and completed the work before Mr. Locus, the boss, returned from his meeting. However, Rossi was in no shape to do the work as well or as quickly as he should have. So you took over a lot of it and just followed his instructions. As a result, it took much longer than usual. Although the machine was back on line by four o'clock, you knew it would have been there at least an hour earlier if Rossi had not taken his long lunch. As everyone at the plant knows, every hour the line is down costs the company about $80,000. You felt guilty about the delay, although you realized it was not your fault.

Normally, this sort of thing would not bother you. But Rossi had also been missing last week, and you covered for him then, too. Moreover, other workers have been complaining about Rossi's erratic behavior for the last six months. You've smelled liquor on his breath more than once, a couple of times at the beginning of the day. Although none of the managers have noticed Rossi's absences, your co-workers figure it is just a matter of time.

As you talked this over with your wife, a psychologist, she frowned and then said that it sounded like Ed Rossi was either an alcoholic or well on his way to becoming one. When she listed the symptoms of alcoholism, you pointed out that Rossi's recent behavior fit the mold pretty well. She then said that the most recent statistics she had seen, which were somewhat outdated, indicated that alcoholics cost U.S. businesses close to $55 billion a year in lost production, health coverage, accidents, crime, and welfare costs. Part of the problem, she explained, was that other workers try to cover up for their friends, and so the problems continue longer than they should.

The next day at work you confronted Rossi tactfully about his behavior and his drinking. You stated that you didn't know for sure that he had a drinking problem but that everyone suspected it. He vehemently denied having a problem with alcohol, and said you were just "up tight" because of yesterday's close call. He reassured you that it would not happen again.

Things went well for about three weeks. Rossi was always on time; you did not smell any liquor on his breath; and he took no more long lunches. But then, when you were assigned, along with Nick Battle and Rossi, to fix a hydraulic lift, Rossi was absent again. There was no way Nick and you could do the job, as it involved holding a large hydraulic piston in place while someone tightened the clamps that held the assembly. Weighing 300 pounds, and awkwardly positioned, the piston required two strong workers to hold it.

"Where's Rossi?" Nick practically bellowed.

"I'll see if I can find him," you responded. This time you went immediately to Jane to ask if Ed had been at lunch with her. She said he hadn't, but she had heard him say he was going over to Gillard's with Paul. Paul said he had lunch with Ed over an hour ago, but that Ed had stayed at Gillard's, saying he was entitled to a three-martini lunch just like the executives. A quick call to Gillard's confirmed Rossi's presence. But this time, speaking on the phone, he refused to return to work, claiming he was sick. By the slurring of his words and his belligerent tone, you figured he was drunk.

"Well, I say it's time to blow the whistle on Mr. Rossi. I'm sick of people covering up for him," Nick said seriously when you told him the situation. "What do you say, are you with me? After all, you've got the facts. Let's get Mr. Locus and get it over with."

Should you go along with Nick? So far, none of the bosses know about Rossi, and may ignore your complaint. Perhaps you owe Rossi one more chance, since you can't be sure he's an alcoholic. But his behavior is starting to affect morale and put you in a bad position. He is definitely costing the company money in lost production time. Consider the options available, the values at stake, and address the problem until it is RESOLVEDD.

□ 12. A Retirement Decision

TERMINATING A LOYAL EMPLOYEE WHOSE PERFORMANCE HAS SLIPPED

You are the division manager of a local subsidiary of a large corporation with its headquarters in the Far West. Your company has eliminated all mandatory retirement policies, following enactment of a state law that guaranteed the right to work for employees of all ages. You have, for the past year, heard disturbing rumors about your oldest shop supervisor. Last spring, some workers complained that he lost a number of their completed job assignment work sheets and then blamed them for not turning in the completed forms after finishing their jobs. This fall, workers have complained that he seems a bit out of touch, rambling on while giving out work assignments and often losing track of which workers are performing which jobs. These rumors have reached your immediate superior, Marlene Worley, the plant superintendent, who has asked you to investigate.

The supervisor in question, Milton Bailey, is 68 years old. He has spent his entire career at your company. When he joined the firm nearly forty-five years ago, it was a small, independent operation that employed less than one-fifth of the workers it does now. In those days, it produced only one-tenth of its present volume, and demanded very little by way of technical management skills. Milt worked his way to the supervisory level on the strength of his ability to work well with small groups of employees in a small department. Since he became a supervisor, Milt's department has doubled in size, and his job has grown to involve a great deal more technical expertise.

Milt's first love is being personally involved with each job. As he says, "I'm a hands-on guy, not some desk jockey." But the increased department size and technical nature of his work have necessarily reduced his personal involvement. In the past, he always received above-average performance reviews and enjoyed the loyalty of his workers. Lately, however, his performance reviews have fallen to an 'adequate' level, and complaints from his subordinates, especially the more recently hired skilled workers, have increased.

Milt has been a model employee throughout his career, always willing to work overtime and use his considerable human relations skills to mediate between management and employees during labor disputes. Moreover, when your company was purchased by the larger conglomerate three years ago, Milt was a moving force in making the transition from independent company to corporate subdivision. It was he who calmed the fears of many workers who worried that the merger meant the loss of their jobs. He strongly supported retaining you in your position after the merger. In fact, he wrote glowing reviews of your work for the new management. In your opinion, the company, the employees, and you personally owe this man a debt of gratitude. It was a keen sense of this debt that led management to make Milt an exception to the mandatory retirement policy still in effect two years ago.

But that was then and now is now, Marlene Worley points out. Gratitude and efficiency are two different things. So you are now observing Milt in action.

When you paid a surprise visit to his area last week, you found his performance competent enough, although he did seem to be a little annoyed and unresponsive to a worker's suggestions about who to assign to a particular job. He also seemed a little distracted and absent-minded, which reminded you of the time he entirely missed a meeting with you for rather vague reasons.

When you mentioned the topic of retirement in the course of a casual conversation with Milt yesterday, he was visibly distressed. At first he insisted, rather defensively, that he would *know* when he no longer had the ability or energy to do his job. He also emphasized that his job is the only important thing in his life since his wife died two years ago.

You are scheduled to meet with Marlene tomorrow morning. She has asked you to consider the possibility of continuing to pay Milt's full salary but giving most of his supervisory responsibilities to a younger person. She has also said the company would give him a substantial bonus if he retired at the end of the current fiscal year. Before taking action, however, she wants your advice and has stated that it will be the single most important factor in her decision.

What should you tell her? Should you do anything about the situation, other than making your report? What does a company owe an employee like Milt? Consider your options, analyzing the situation until it is RESOLVEDD.

☐ 13. Build to Suit

CAN YOU AFFORD TO HIRE A DISABLED WORKER?

Marcia Yellow Eagle was clearly the best qualified applicant you had interviewed in the last two weeks. You were looking for a good architect to add to your construction company, but you also knew the costs of hiring Ms. Yellow Eagle.

Marcia was the first candidate you interviewed. She impressed you with her résumé and letters of recommendation. She had a master's degree from one of the top three schools of architecture in the nation, six years of experience with two well-known architects, and more training in structural engineering than most architects had. No other candidate came close to these qualifications.

However, there was a drawback: Marcia was unable to walk, and sat in a wheelchair. She explained that she could use her crutches to get around a bit, but that she seldom bothered, as she was very comfortable getting around in her wheelchair. But you did not see her disability as the problem—the problem was, ironically, architectural.

When Marcia said that she had a very hard time getting to your office for her interview, she expressed some surprise that a construction company would occupy a building that did not have any access for wheelchairs. You explained that the building was over sixty years old and that you had never employed anyone who used a wheelchair before. She said she understood, but also said that if she were to accept this job, there would have to be an elevator and other structural changes made. Without such changes, she would simply not accept a job with your firm.

Being an architect, she was able to explain exactly what was needed. And as a construction company owner, you knew exactly what such modifications would cost. To install the elevator, alter the existing building to accommodate it, plus the other necessary adaptations, would run over $200,000. When you asked Marcia if she would consider starting before the modifications were made, she said yes. But unless they were done within a few months, she added, she would have to quit.

At that point in the interview process, you told her that you would weigh her requests when considering whom to hire, but that she was still one of your top candidates. Now, however, it is clear that she is the only candidate any reasonable employer would consider. The other three candidates are good but nowhere near Marcia in ability or experience.

Without the need to modify your building, which you own, there would be no doubt about who to hire. At this point, however, it just doesn't look like you can afford the modifications. But can you afford to let Marcia slip through your fingers? Then there is always the possibility of a lawsuit for discriminating against the disabled, though perhaps no one would ever know why you decided not to hire Marcia.

You know that Marcia could add so much to your company that it seems foolish not to hire her. But your treasurer has explained that an expenditure of $200,000 right now would place the company on very thin ice for at least a year. A major financial setback or lost contract could put you in the red. Deep down you know that if you don't hire Marcia, the reason would be solely because she was disabled; or rather, that because she was disabled you could not afford to hire her. But aren't these really the same? There is simply no way to look at this as a black-and-white decision. It is a decision that requires thought to be RESOLVEDD.

☐ 14. It's His Company, But . . .

GENDER DISCRIMINATION AND A PROMOTION

John Damien is the president of a medium-sized printing company that he started from scratch over twenty years ago. Rachel Besset has worked for John's company for the last four years, and has reached a turning point in her career. At the present executive meeting, she is being considered for promotion to vice president. If promoted, she would be the first woman to reach that level in the company. However, a struggle is brewing.

Rachel began four years ago as a salesperson, dealing mostly with small clients and companies that were placing a single order. She prided herself on treating everyone as if they were long-time customers. As a result, many of the new clients did become steady customers. Rachel's sales expertise increased John's business substantially in the next two years.

During the last two years, Rachel continued to sell printing but also took over a good deal of the office management at the print shop. John had always been a bit disorganized when it came to the details of everyday operations. Rachel began helping with one or two loose ends and went on to cover more and more of the everyday business of the company. John was increasingly freed to work with the printers and graphics art department, his two specialties. Eventually, on your recommendation, John made her office manager, with a raise and bonus.

Although she rarely worked directly with John, who was hardly ever in the office, John trusted your judgment enough to promote her. The company is now running much more efficiently.

At the last executive meeting, you proposed that Rachel be promoted to the rank of vice president. You gave a positive presentation that the other three executives found convincing. John, however, spoke up, abruptly opposing it. Because of his position as president, John's opposition was a veto.

The other executives joined you in objecting to John's veto. As a result, John said that he would consider it for a week and announce his decision at the next meeting. That meeting took place earlier today, and you are still reeling from it all.

John began the meeting by explaining that he just could not promote Rachel. He was not, he insisted, biased against women. He explained, however, that he had never been able to work closely with women without becoming nervous and inhibited in his job. That was the reason there had never been another female executive. He apologized for seeming to be sexist, explaining that it was not a prejudice, but a simple fact: a phobia according to his therapist. Indeed, he explained, his feelings ran so deep that even therapy had failed to improve his ability to work with women. Since he would have to work closely with any vice president on major issues, he could not take the chance of promoting Rachel. If he could not work effectively, the business would suffer.

You had argued, at the meeting, that in her new capacity Rachel would not be doing much more than in the past. John had responded that she would be at weekly meetings, be consulted on all major contracts and negotiations, and meet with him regularly for all kinds of things that vice presidents do. At that point, you had suggested just giving her the promotion and raise, without any new responsibilities and without her having to attend the weekly meetings. John pointed out that it would be bad business to pay for a vice president who did no more than an office manager. In addition, it would be bad for her morale to promote her to executive level without executive responsibilities or privileges. It was better, he said, not to promote her, especially since she didn't know that she was being considered. "No harm, no foul," was the way he put it. "Just keep the whole thing confidential, and no one gets upset."

Nothing you said could change John's mind. Although you think this is unfair to Rachel, you can hardly blame John. After all, you think, it isn't exactly his fault. It's a psychological problem he is trying to overcome, and he deserves credit for that much. At first, you concur with John's explanation that he is not prejudiced—he is going on past experience. And the business surely would suffer if John couldn't do his job efficiently. But you were still troubled by your conviction that Rachel deserved the promotion and could do more for the company if she received it.

As you were walking out of the meeting, Rachel stopped you and asked to speak with you in private.

"I heard a rumor that something big concerning me was coming up at the meeting today," she said.

"I can't discuss the meeting at all, Rachel," you said. "These meetings are private. Execs only, you know." The excuse sounded weak even as you said it.

Rachel picked up on your uneasiness and kept asking about what had gone on and how it affected her. She said that if she were being discussed, for better or worse, she had a right to know. What should you say to her—today, tomorrow, or later?

She does not accept the claim of confidentiality. She pointed out that you yourself hinted strongly that something important would happen to her. Should you tell her what happened? How could you explain it, if you did? Could she have grounds for a lawsuit? Suppose she asked you to testify against John? There are so many awkward and troublesome events that you could be caught up in. And how would John react to your act of "betrayal"? What do you owe John, the company, and Rachel? Much will have to be sorted through before you can make a responsible decision and have the situation RESOLVEDD.

☐ 15. Lose It or Move It

IS BEING OVERWEIGHT A REASON FOR DISCHARGE?

Darrien worked as an emergency room nurse at Bigtown Hospital until she was suspended pending the decision by a three-member board of review. The hospital has arranged for a hearing to help the board determine whether or not she should be terminated. You have been asked to serve on the board of review as the representative of Darrien's peer group.

You have been a registered nurse at Bigtown for almost eight years and have a nodding acquaintance with Darrien. You do not, however, work with her or know her except to say "Hi" in the halls. The other members of the board are Lord, a staff surgeon, and Hines, a senior administrator from the personnel department.

The problem before the board involves Darrien's weight. She is 5 feet 5 inches tall and weighs 330 pounds. When she began at Bigtown Hospital four years ago, she had weighed 240 pounds. During her pre-employment interviews, she had stated that she had lost 30 pounds during her senior year as a nursing student because her school had a limit on how much a nursing student could weigh. The school had taken the position that some nursing functions require that nurses be physically fit. Moving patients and administering cardiopulmonary resuscitation (CPR), for example, require strength and agility. Darrien had failed to pass her physical during her senior year and had agreed to go on a school-supervised weight loss program, during which she lost the 30 pounds the school regulations required.

After her graduation, she joined the nursing staff at Bigtown and began to regain the weight she had lost. Now, four years later, she weighs 330 pounds, despite being put on a hospital-administered weight control program over nine months before.

The hospital, like the school of nursing, has strict physical fitness requirements for its staff. Darrien is nowhere near the weight guidelines for someone her height. The hospital rules require her to weigh 230 pounds or less, and she had been hired with the understanding that she would lose weight. During her weight loss program, however, she gained 45 pounds. The hospital administration has decided that Darrien cannot perform her job effectively due to the limits on her physical endurance and mobility caused by her weight. The administration has stated that Darrien was granted sufficient time to lose the necessary weight and has failed, and it is now appropriate that she be terminated. The termination order has been submitted to the three-member board of review as required by the nurses' contract.

During the early testimony to the board, the hospital lawyer argued that Darrien had violated her contractual obligations to maintain her fitness for duty and that therefore the hospital no longer had any obligation to honor her contract, which runs for another eight months. Furthermore, the lawyer pointed out that her weight prevents her from performing her duties adequately in the emergency room, where she works. On a couple of occasions, she became faint and breathless during particularly long emergency CPR sessions, which lasted almost an hour each. In each case, another nurse took over her job while she rested.

The hospital lawyer further argued that the hospital has an obligation to its patients to maintain high standards of performance for its staff. In addition, some nurses who testified thought that it might be best for Darrien to avoid work that makes such heavy physical demands. Thus, perhaps everyone would benefit in the long run from her being released.

Darrien argues, however, that she is fit for her job and is being discriminated against because of a social stigma attached to overweight people. She claims that forty-five minutes of CPR would exhaust any members of the board and that many trim, fit nurses cannot go that long without a break. Darrien maintains that she has substantially performed her contractual obligations. As far as the violation of her obligation to lose weight, Darrien believes that she is an addictive personality and cannot stop eating because of a genetic condition that is beyond her control.

You are aware of recent studies indicating that some people suffer from the sort of condition Darrien describes. Moreover, some researchers have described such a condition and classified it as a disease like alcoholism. She believes that since she has no control over her weight, the hospital is punishing her for something she is not responsible for, thus violating her right to just and fair treatment. But you are not at all sure that Darrien falls into this category, because she has not presented any evidence to back up her claim.

After the hearings and discussion, Lord votes to keep Darrien on staff until the end of her eight-month contract; if she loses the weight, he will vote to give her a new contract; if not, he recommends another hearing. Hines votes for termination, rejecting the idea that Darrien has no control over her weight. Even if the claim were true, Hines says, the fact remains that Darrien had not passed the physical required for continued employment. She adds, "Our obligations are to the patients first, and if she isn't fit enough to do her job, the patients suffer." You ask for some time to think before voting.

Yours will be the deciding vote, and you have the evening to think it over. Taking all pertinent values and possible consequences into account, what would be best? Analyze the case until it is RESOLVEDD.

☐ 16. Make Up or Break Up?
PERSONAL APPEARANCE AND COMPANY POLICY

You had been working as a travel agent for more than a year. You couldn't believe it when you first got the pink slip in your paycheck envelope. You had been fired! What amazed you even more was that the cause was your refusal to wear makeup on the job. Now you are trying to decide whether to sue your former employer.

You have been talking recently to representatives of the Americans for a Free Workplace (AFFW), a group similar to the American Civil Liberties Union. The AFFW had contacted you to encourage you to pursue a lawsuit for wrongful discharge.

To think, this had happened when all you had wanted was a nice job at a travel agency, to earn a little money, meet people, and work part time so you'd have time to spend at home with Christine, your 3-year-old daughter. At first the whole thing seemed silly, but as you thought about it, you realized there were a number of important rights and principles at stake.

You took the part-time (twenty-five hours a week) job as a travel agent with Cheapo Travel Agency over a year before, partly because it seemed to be a moderate-sized corporation (250 employees at ten national locations) with a sense of humor. "Just look at their name," you had thought when noting the employment ad in the paper. During your interview, it seemed like just the place you were looking for. The managers you had talked to did have a sense of humor, had no disagreement at all with your working part time, nor with juggling your schedule to fit the needs of your daughter. They especially liked your previous experience as a real estate salesperson and your manner of dealing with people. They hired you right on the spot.

An employee group, not a union, asked you to join despite the fact that you were only part time and not really eligible for membership. This group did not negotiate contracts or require dues but did consult with management in making policies for the agency and its workers. It was the action of this employee group, however, that led to your firing.

The group had agreed with management that the company's image needed to be improved, to have a more glamorous and "European" feel. Most of the improvements were matters of changing the names of vacation packages to sound more European, the decor of the offices, and other rather superficial measures. However, at the suggestion of the employee group's female officers, the company had adopted an appearance standard that included the rule that women employees who deal directly with the public must wear "at least a minimum amount of makeup." Male employees were required to wear suits and ties that reflected current European fashion standards.

You had refused to wear makeup, saying that you had never worn it in your life, and were not about to start at 36 years of age. On stating your refusal, you had been asked to meet with a committee composed of management and representatives of the employee group. During the meeting, you explained that you had nothing against makeup or people who wore it but didn't use it yourself and didn't wish to start using it. One of the managers, Mike Redstone, explained that the policy was meant simply to present a "continental European look" to the customers, giving them a flavor of the style and elegance of France, where most women were known to wear makeup. He added that this was the reason the male employees would wear "French-style" suits and ties. Marge Doctrowe, the employee group's president, told you that the idea for the makeup rule came from the group's executive council, which had suggested the idea to management.

"It was our choice, you see, and you are a member of the group, so you shouldn't look at this as something the company forced on you," Marge concluded.

"Do you think I don't look good enough to sell European vacation plans? Don't I have a right to dress and look the way I want to look, so long as it isn't outrageous or harmful to business?" you asked.

Everyone in the group had responded that you are a highly professional worker and an attractive representative of the company. They all agreed, however, that the rule must apply to everyone. When you again declined to adopt the policy, Mike offered you a job confirming reservations and flights, a phone job behind the scenes, but at your normal salary and work schedule. Following your second refusal, the meeting was terminated.

A week later, the pink slip appeared in your pay envelope. You then filed a formal grievance. But the grievance review committee, composed primarily of the same people you had met with earlier, denied the appeal. One member, Bart Lincoln, had been adamant in his defense of your personal autonomy. He argued that requiring makeup seemed to be left over from the old days when "women were expected to be glamorous even on the job."

You suspected that Bart had contacted the AFFW's lawyers, who then contacted you to encourage you to file suit for wrongful discharge. The AFFW lawyer, Michelle Permenter, argued that you should file suit because this is an issue of women's choice and privacy, a matter not just of personal autonomy, but of the rights and freedoms of all women workers. You are not sure you want to go this far, but you do recognize the larger issues beyond your own case.

Should you file the suit? Is this really a serious rights issue, or are you just being stubborn? Are you bound by the rules freely adopted by the employee group and presented by it to management? What are the central issues? How should you react? Analyze the case until it is RESOLVEDD.

☐ 17. A Fair Handicap?
QUALIFICATIONS, SENIORITY, AND AFFIRMATIVE ACTION

You are on a five-member panel assigned to review three workers' files for a promotion decision. The company you work for has a policy of worker participation in hiring, promotion, and firing decisions that was implemented as part of its union contract. The panel also includes another fellow union employee, a salaried worker, a member of management, and the director of personnel. And—just your luck—the situation is a sticky one.

Three union members are applying for promotion to the position of production-line supervisor. Dale Riggs, Martha Gale, and Marcus Washington were all hired at about the same time, with Dale having two weeks' seniority over Martha, and Martha about 8 days' seniority over Marcus. All three have been employed as line workers on the same assembly line, and each is considered a valuable worker.

Marcus is a black man, hired under the company's affirmative action program. This program was voluntarily instituted by the company. The union advocated the program and made concessions in order to get it adopted by the company. The union agreed to downplay seniority in the promotion process in order to further the goals of affirmative action.

Since Dale and Martha have seniority and Marcus is a member of a racial minority, promoting either Dale or Martha may be taken as upholding seniority and thus as a compromise of the affirmative action policy. But although seniority may be overruled for the sake of affirmative action, seniority is still a time-honored and important principle for the union. It must not be taken too lightly nor ignored completely. The union wants seniority to remain as important as any other requirement for promotion. In the eyes of the union, a compromise of seniority might set a dangerous precedent, because management would like to drop seniority altogether as a criterion for promotion.

Can you apply either affirmative action guidelines or seniority in the case without being unfair to someone? You don't think so. You wonder if therefore Martha is a good compromise candidate.

During the discussion of the candidates, it is generally agreed that, judging by their performance, all are well qualified for the promotion. However, the other panel members believe that Dale is slightly better qualified than Martha, who is slightly better qualified than Marcus. However, no one on the panel believes the differences in their job performance are significant. Although everyone likes and respects Dale and Martha, Marcus seems to interact best with the other workers and managers. His congeniality could be a real asset in performing his job. You are fairly sure, though, that Dale and Martha are almost equally easy to work with.

The preliminary vote shows that one panel member firmly believes that Dale is entitled to the promotion because he has done the best work of the three and has slightly more seniority. Another member clearly favors Marcus on grounds of affirmative action. A third member wants to promote Martha because her qualifications seem slightly better than Marcus's, though less than Dale's and, she says, because women are underrepresented in supervisory roles in the plant. In addition, she says, Title VII of the Civil Rights Act indicates that, like racial minorities, women are a protected class covered by affirmative action guidelines.

Your fellow union employee and you are concerned about the whole situation and believe in the seniority principle, giving Dale the edge. But you also believe that a matter of a few days seems largely insignificant when considering such an important promotion. Furthermore, you both recognize that to abandon the affirmative action policy, adopted after a long fight on the union's part, would send the wrong message to black employees, who are also underrepresented in supervisory roles. You realize that affirmative action covers both Marcus and Martha, but also that the company has never discriminated against women, while it has a poor record of hiring and promoting black workers. Yet Marcus was hired with affirmative action in place, and you wonder if that's all he's entitled to, or whether affirmative action applies to every decision involving him from now on. The other union panelist says she will abide by your decision since you've been at the company as a union employee for almost twenty-five years.

How can you best decide the case? Which principles play the most important role in the case: seniority, performance, or affirmative action? The union's contract stipulates that none of the three can be ignored and seems to indicate that they are of roughly equal importance. Are there other considerations to be taken into account? Analyze the case until it is RESOLVEDD.

☐ 18. Is This Norming?

GOVERNMENT AFFIRMATIVE ACTION POLICY AND THE RIGHT TO KNOW

This is your first day on the job at the State Department of Unemployment. Your boss, Hakeem Gilmore, is showing you the ropes. At present, he is showing you how to respond to a company's request for a job applicant's test scores. Job applicants often go through the state office, taking tests and obtaining referrals for job interviews. All this is required in order to receive state unemployment compensation.

The applicant in this case is an Hispanic male. You have looked up the list of scores for the exam in question and are now verifying the score for the present applicant. You find his name on the list in the front of the file for the appropriate exam. You see the number 300 next to it.

"What's his score?" Hakeem asks.

"300," you answer.

"Oh, you've got the wrong list. That's not the score we report to employers, that's just his raw score on the exam. We don't report raw scores."

You are a little confused; "What do we report, then?"

Hakeem turns the file folder around and flips through a few pages until he finds a yellow sheet of paper. The title at the top of the sheet reads, "Adjusted Scores: Exam 76/1989". "Here's his score," Hakeem says, "It's 67. Write '67' down in the space on your form there."

As you do so, you ask, "What does '67' mean? 67 percent?"

"Not exactly. It's his adjusted score once we factor his ethnic group into the equation. Haven't you heard about racial and ethnic norming?"

"No. What is it?"

Hakeem explains that ever since the Carter administration, state and federal employment agencies have adjusted scores on the basis of race and ethnic group for purposes of affirmative action. He shows you the list of raw scores and then the list of adjusted scores for the same exam. You notice that "HM" is typed next to your applicant's name, "WF" next to another, and "BM" next to a third.

"I take it these mean—what?—Hispanic male, black male, and white female?" you ask.

"Now you've got it," Hakeem replies.

Next to the names of these three people, you find the raw score listed as 300. But on the adjusted list, the score next to the Hispanic male's name is 67, the black male's is 83, and the white female's is 44.

"Wait a minute," you exclaim, "You mean I have to report a 67 for one guy, a 44 for the woman, and an 83 for another guy? Their scores on the exam were identical. That isn't fair."

"Sure it is. These scores take into account past prejudice, the educations received by different racial groups, and other discriminatory factors. You aren't going to tell me that some white suburban school doesn't give a better education than an inner-city black school, are you?" Hakeem responds.

"Well . . ."

"Look, the Carter administration figured out the formula for converting the scores based on just those kinds of factors. The reasoning is that if the Hispanic guy scored 300, he had to have more on the ball than a white guy who scored 300. The reason he didn't score better was probably that he had lousy schooling. The white guy had superior training, but didn't do any better. So the Hispanic guy must be smarter to begin with. Obviously he's been held back by poor education. The formula factors this in," Hakeem explains patiently.

You see the point. Hakeem is right. On the average, inner-city schools don't have the money, facilities, or even the books that schools in richer, white districts have. There is something to say for an inner-city kid who overcomes these problems, which aren't his or her fault, and does as well as someone trained at a better school. But then again, how do you know that the white female on the list did, in fact, attend a superior high school and that the other two attended poor inner-city schools? And how do you weigh an inner-city black school against an Hispanic one so as to get a ratio of 83 to 67? This seems impossible to establish. But then, you are not the expert.

"OK, I get the idea. So where do I write 'adjusted scores'?"

"Nowhere, man. You just report them."

"You mean the employer never knows we're doing this? They don't get a list of raw scores, and we don't tell them these are 'doctored' numbers?" you ask in amazement.

"That's the policy. Take it or leave it."

You are very concerned about this answer. It seems like lying or deception. Doesn't the employer have a right to full information about the test scores? Apart from all the other issues, this just seems like biased reporting. Whether the employer has discriminated against anyone, whether the agency must comply with affirmative action policies, or whether the candidates deserve a special consideration does not alter the fact that this is deceptive.

"Mr. Gilmore, I just can't do this. I don't have any problems with the aims of the program. In fact, I strongly support the idea of affirmative action. But this is just deception. The employers are not receiving accurate information, and can't determine from our figures if the applicants are suitable for the jobs. Surely, the employers have a right to know the raw scores and then decide on the basis of their own judgment."

"That isn't your concern. Your job is to report the adjusted scores. That's all. The policy is almost fifteen years old, and there have been no complaints about it. Our job is to follow policy. If you can't handle that, maybe you should quit."

Is this the answer? Should you quit or just report the results as required? Should you blow the whistle somehow? Maybe you should find a way of letting employers know what's going on. Then again, there is a lot of discrimination still going on in America, and education is far from equal. But is this a proper way to compensate? Are all these factors important, or should you just do your job as instructed? Your problem is how to answer these questions so it can be RESOLVEDD.

☐ 19. Is This Doctor Sick?

AIDS TESTING FOR DOCTORS, HONESTY, AND PERSONAL LOYALTY

You couldn't believe it when your brother, Carl, told you that he had just tested HIV-positive! You knew, of course, that Carl was gay. But you thought that since he was a doctor, there would be little chance he would become infected with the AIDS virus. Carl had tried to ease your fears with the information that ongoing studies of HIV-infected people indicated about a one in three chance that they would actually contract full-blown AIDS. You had read, though, that the studies were far from complete, and that according to some experts 100 percent of HIV-infected people would get AIDS.

This is a long-term worry. However, there is a more immediate problem. You work in Carl's office as the office manager. Twelve people, including two other doctors, four nurses, two receptionists, and two

X-ray technicians, also work there. The problem is that Carl has asked you not to tell anyone at the office of his test results. "We especially can't let the patients find out," he had said.

"But Carl, the AMA (American Medical Association) has required HIV-infected doctors to disclose their condition," you protested.

"Not quite. What the AMA says is that it is unethical for someone like me not to inform the patients of the condition. Well, ethics cuts two ways here. The AMA is just reacting to AIDS fears and antigay sentiments in the country. Most other conditions, even highly infectious ones, do not require disclosure. What does that tell you? Then there's my privacy. This information is between me and my doctor. My medical history is my private business just as much as my sexual preference," Carl answers.

"That's true, but AIDS is 100 percent fatal. What about 'Do no harm'? Isn't that one of the primary ethical obligations of a physician?"

"First," he replied, "I haven't got AIDS. Second, there's a chance I'll never develop it. Third, I'm an internist, not a surgeon. Even if I were, the statistics indicate that the chances of a patient getting infected during surgery are about 0.0065 in a million. Not exactly a high risk, even in surgery. Imagine how low the risk is for nonsurgical contacts," Carl says, rather angrily. "Besides, I'm asking you, as my brother, to keep this confidential. Believe me, when I feel it's a significant danger, I'll tell every patient we have."

"That's a bit tough on me, Carl. I am the office manager, remember. Don't I have a duty to tell the rest of the staff? At least they should know."

"And if they blurt it out to a patient? Do you know how many ridiculous lawsuits we'd get from patients who have a cold and are convinced it's AIDS? Not to mention former patients who haven't seen me in years and who come down with something, or even test HIV-positive for reasons totally unconnected with us? I've told you because I trust you. Let's just keep this in the family."

For all the reasons you had mentioned, you are deeply concerned about your brother's request. Then again, Carl is right about the nature of the minuscule risks involved. The AMA's position is probably overly conservative and may well be formulated just to promote the public image of the profession. Moreover, the AMA has no legal control over a doctor. Many doctors do not belong to the AMA, which is a voluntary professional organization. Finally, no federal or state laws require disclosure. But you still cannot shake the feeling that this is a fact patients have a right to know and make up their own minds about.

In going over some literature on HIV and AIDS, you find that Carl's estimates of the chances of getting infected from a doctor are correct, maybe even too high. The chances may be as little as 0.00065 in a million—for surgical patients. The chances must be even more astronomical for noninvasive procedures. Carl does perform some minor outpatient surgery in the office but rarely does more than removing stitches and lancing boils. The statistics indicate, however, that only between 0.3 and 3 patients in a thousand whose blood is infected by the blood of a surgeon who has HIV will contract HIV. These are very long odds.

So, you wonder, if the chances of Carl infecting a patient are so low, shouldn't I honor his request? He is my brother, and he did tell me about this as his brother, not doctor to office manager. Family loyalty is a precious commodity. But so is patient trust. You talk to dozens of patients a week who trust you, Carl, and the whole practice to do your very best for them. Don't you owe them something? If only this AIDS epidemic were not such a political football. There is too much misunderstanding and hysteria involved, so maybe Carl is right. But this is not merely a political decision, for there are lives involved.

You wonder if your worries will ever be RESOLVEDD and the basis of your decision clarified. But you must decide, and then must live with the results.

☐ 20. Worth the Effort?

HANDLING SEXUAL HARASSMENT

Violet Spear had done her homework. But then, she felt she had to in order to know whether or not she should file a grievance against her colleague, Theo Lucasey. Violet did not want to jeopardize her job as a junior marketing executive by appearing to be a "bad sport," "overly sensitive woman," or any "hysterical female." Theo had called her all of these in the last few months when she complained to him about his conduct toward her.

Violet was trying to find out whether the way Theo had been treating her constituted sexual harassment. What she found out was interesting. First, she looked for the legal guidelines for sexual harassment. Under Title VII of the 1964 Civil Rights Act, sexual harassment is defined as

Unwelcome sexual advances, requests for sexual favors, and other verbal or physical conduct of a sexual nature constitute sexual harassment when (1) submission to such conduct is made either explicitly or implicitly a term or condition of an individual's employment, (2) submission to or rejection of such conduct by an individual is used as the basis for employment decisions affecting such individual, or (3) such conduct has the purpose or effect of unreasonably interfering with an individual's work performance or creating an intimidating, hostile, or offensive working environment.*

This seemed pretty clear to Violet and seemed to definitely apply to the way Theo had been treating her.

Violet is very successful in her marketing position. She attributes part of her success to the fact that her clients trust her professionalism as well as her knowledge of her job. Part of what Violet sees as important to her professional image is her wardrobe: she dresses in very conservative business suits that are feminine yet reassuring to her conservative male clients. Before Theo's remarks, no one had ever referred to her wardrobe as anything but tasteful or stylish.

Theo was transferred from a regional branch about six months earlier and almost immediately began to make comments to Violet whenever they worked together. At first it had just been things like "Very nice suit," but soon he began to add a growl or a low barking noise to his comments. She had called him on this right away, but he accused her of being overly sensitive. The comments continued and gradually became more suggestive. Again Violet told him to keep his comments to himself. He responded by accusing her of being a bad sport.

The situation reached its peak about a week ago when once again Theo made a comment about her clothes: "That suit is so sexy I can't stand it. Why don't we go into my office where you can take it off so I can get some work done? You know what kind of work I mean, right?"

Violet replied angrily, "Why don't you just knock it off. Act like a grown man instead of a 14-year-old with a hormone problem. I simply will not tolerate these remarks any more. One more and I'm going to have to file a complaint."

"Don't be a hysterical female, dear. Those business suits of yours

---

* "Guidelines on Discrimination on the Basis of Sex" (Washington, DC: Equal Employment Opportunity Commission, November 10, 1980).

really turn me on. I've always had a thing for women who dress in those 'power suits.' I like power. Why not just stop wearing those clothes? Maybe then I'll be able to control myself," was Theo's response.

Violet had walked away in disgust. In the next week she looked up the harassment guidelines and talked to a number of women at her office about what had happened. When she asked what to do, the replies were not encouraging. One woman said it couldn't be harassment, because Theo wasn't her boss and had no power over her employment. Another said that she had no confidence that any of the male executives would take her complaints seriously. A third said that unless one of the male executives actually witnessed the harassment, nothing would be done. In all, five different women expressed the sentiment that no male executive would take her seriously, and probably they'd believe Theo's comment about her being overly sensitive or hysterical.

"It's the way men are. Must be genetic. No government guidelines are going to reverse 41,000 years of habit," one had said.

Violet was confused. The terms of the guidelines seemed to cover Theo's actions—work was becoming oppressive. Yet she had gotten no encouragement from other women at the company. She had also come across some statistics that stated that 67 percent of the women who complained of harassment lost their jobs within one year, either by being fired or by voluntarily leaving. The same source stated that only 9 percent of the complaints ever resulted in the harassment ceasing. There was a procedure for sexual harassment claims at Violet's firm, but each step of the process involved some male executive who might react just as the other women predicted.

Violet is afraid of being labeled a complainer or a troublemaker. She began to think Theo's comments might be correct, maybe if she just stopped wearing those suits he'd leave her alone. She didn't want to compromise her career; she had worked too hard and been too professional to give it up for a jerk like Theo. But her clients responded well to her professional style of dressing and had never insulted her like Theo. Would they be bothered by a switch in her wardrobe? Yet if she didn't complain, work would continue to be oppressive, and there was no telling how many other women Theo would insult. Violet has to make a decision about how she's going to get this problem RESOLVEDD. Put yourself in her position to complete the analysis and reach a decision.

❑ 21. A Warranted Grievance?

A PERSONAL CONFLICT ON THE JOB

You have been working at the desk next to Bill for six months, and until recently things had been going pretty well. He seemed like a friendly guy, always seemed ready to help you, and often came over to your lunchroom table to talk. But all that changed quickly a few days ago.

It had been a warm weekend and you had gone to a baseball game to see the local team play the Chicago Cubs. Being an old Chicagoan, you were pleased to see the Cubs win 9–1, although you did feel a twinge of guilt for cheering against the home team. All in all, though, it was a great break from work, and last Monday you were telling everyone at your lunch table about the game when Bill came over with his lunch tray. He sat down and listened to you talk about the game for a few minutes and then said, "You mean you're actually a Cub fan? I can't believe it. You seem like a fairly rational and normal person, too."

"Well, I was raised in Chicago, and the Cubs have always been my favorite team," you answered with a laugh. "And it isn't all that often that we Cub fans get to see them win."

"What a backbiting SOB!" Bill then said rather loudly.

"What? Don't get all worked up, it's just a baseball game!" you responded quickly.

"Maybe, but only a real SOB could cheer against our local boys. The kind of a person who roots for the Cubs is the kind of person who can't be trusted."

At first, you thought he was just kidding. Then you noticed the looks on the faces of the other two people at the lunch table and had second thoughts. They looked at each other, nodded, and then abruptly got up and left. You found out later that they had seen Bill get this way before and knew that nothing would likely improve the situation. He was serious, and arguing with him would just make more trouble.

Not knowing this at the time, however, you proceeded to defend yourself. His responses clearly became more hostile, until you realized that you were both becoming very loud and very nasty. By the time you were finally getting ready to leave, Bill had questioned your ability to do your job, and your loyalty to the company and had insulted your family. Bill was so upset that he abruptly arose, dumped his lunch tray in your lap, threw his chair to the floor, and practically ran out of the lunch room.

As you sat there stunned and extremely angry, Marianne Dawson came over and sat down across from you. She told you that Bill is known for this kind of emotional outbreak. By now, though, everyone had assumed he'd gotten over this kind of thing and had perhaps received some counseling. "Try to smooth things over as soon as you can, any way you can, or he'll make your life miserable," she said, "I've seen it before."

"At least he's not my boss," you thought. "I'd hate to have to work for the guy after this. Maybe I can patch things up later on." You were hoping that when you returned from the meeting you had outside the office that afternoon, Bill would have calmed down so you could straighten things out.

By 3:30, you had returned to your desk. Bill was not there, but you noticed that all your file trays had been dumped upside down onto your desk. As you were staring at the mess, Bill returned and said, laughingly, "What a damn slob you are. I was right about you all along. A no-good worker if I ever saw one." You were no longer in a mood to be forgiving at that point.

"You're a jerk, Bill. Stay away from my desk or else."

"Or else what, you traitor?" Bill shouted. At this point you saw he was out of control, so you quickly left. A short while later, when you saw that Bill had left the office, you went back to work. But it cost you an extra hour to straighten up the papers on your desk.

Over the next few days there was no repeat of the dumping incident. But every time Bill saw you he made some nasty comment. In fact, it was so difficult to work at your desk that you began to work at a desk across the office whose occupant was on vacation. Once you did that, Bill left you alone. But whenever you tried to use your own desk, he started in on you again. It became clear in the next few days that there wasn't even a chance to work things out, Bill would just cut you off in mid-sentence.

By now you have talked with a number of people about this problem and learned that no one is willing to back you up. The reason is that whenever anyone complained about Bill in the past, it got nowhere. It seems that the vice president in charge of your area, who is very much like Bill, always backs Bill or simply tells everyone that personal problems are not his concern. He has said that Bill is a good worker, with ten years at the company, and that if anyone is to go, it won't be

Bill. At least three people told you to work out an exchange of desks to get away from Bill. However, no one at all would make the change.

All the strain makes it very difficult for you to look forward to going to work each day. A part of you, though, feels that it must be your fault for not being able to work things out with Bill. After all, anyone with a college education like yours should be able to deal with Bill. In fact, you would like to avoid talking to anyone in upper management because you are afraid they will think you can't handle your job if you cry to them about a silly situation like this.

But what did you do to deserve this persecution? And why should you work at least an hour overtime every night as a result of staying away from the office to avoid Bill's attacks on you? You know the situation cannot go on and that something must be done.

There is a formal company grievance procedure, but do you want to use it for your personal problems? Besides, the person in charge of the grievance committee is none other than Bill's vice president friend. To make matters worse, the only person you could possibly appeal to is the president of the company, who is rarely in town, is very busy when she is, and who has a reputation for having little patience with employees who can't solve personal problems. Quitting seems too drastic, and it would mean taking a sizable cut in salary even if you made a lateral transfer to another company. How should the situation be RESOLVEDD?

☐ 22. Who Stays, Who Goes?
A WORKING COUPLE WITH A SICK CHILD

"I can't stay with Tommy, dear. I stayed home the last time he was sick. We have a deal, right? We take turns on these things," your spouse says to you in the course of a 7:30 A.M. discussion. Your 3-year-old son is running a mild fever and has been complaining of a stomach ache since late last night. It may be nothing serious, but someone has to stay with him, because the day care center has been closed by a measles epidemic.

"I know, I know, but there are fifty students today who are expecting me to be there to go over their study questions for the final exam on Friday. How many people are waiting for *you* at school?" is your response.

"Oh, right! Just because I'm still a student and you're a teacher, I'm the one whose work can wait. You know that Professor Lehrer is hell on wheels when someone misses an exam. In case you forgot, my final exam is today, not Friday. Don't you remember when you had Lehrer in grad school? I'll never get a makeup exam. Grad school isn't like undergrad—no breaks."

You remember quite well. Professor Lehrer almost flunked you out of grad school four years earlier when you were completing your master's degree, and just because you missed a couple of regular classes. What would have happened if you had missed the final exam? You don't like to think about it.

"Can't you get someone to do the review for you? Your fifty students just want the review. It doesn't have to be you who gives it, does it?"

You think for a moment. "Yes, it does. Everyone else who could do it has classes of their own at those times. I'm the only one teaching Calculus II this semester. There's no one else around who'd be ready to do it. I owe it to my students to be there. They count on me."

"Look," says your spouse, "my whole grade for this class is riding on the final exam, three hours from now. And here you are arguing with me about your duty to people you're not even related to. I can't believe it."

"Too bad your parents are out of town this week. Why do they have to take their vacations in May? Why can't they wait 'til school's out?" An unfair question, you know, but you couldn't help asking.

"They take it now to avoid all the people with kids who go in June. What a dumb question!"

Things are getting out of hand rapidly. Wanting to avoid a major argument, you say, "Let's try to get this particular problem resolved now. Later we can work on an emergency plan for the future."

How can you address the problem in a way that is fair to both of you? What ethical values are at stake here? What are your options? Can you design a plan that would likely resolve such future problems, as well? Analyze the case until it is RESOLVEDD.

☐ 23. Two Minutes Too Late
IS YOUR CO-WORKER BEING FAIRLY TREATED?

"All that for two minutes?" you thought. It did not seem fair to you, and you could tell that it did not seem fair to the other three secretaries who shared your area.

Lashondra had arrived at work two minutes late this morning, and her boss, Kendra Carroll, was waiting at her desk when she came in. You and the other secretaries knew this was going to be trouble. You had seen it before. Lashondra had not, since she had been working in your area for only two weeks following her transfer. Surely, she had not confronted this kind of hassle working for Tom Dryden in the downstairs office.

Kendra shouted, "We don't pay you for not being here! Tom Dryden might have, but I won't."

Lashondra didn't have time to say anything before Kendra dropped the largest stack of file folders you had ever seen onto her desk. "Finish typing the cover letters for all of these by noon or else," Kendra snarled. "And I don't want any of the rest of you to touch a single folder, type a single letter, or help this slacker in any way, or you'll have twice as much work to do as she does." The door slammed as Kendra went back into her office.

The look on Lashondra's face was a mix of astonishment and deep anguish. There was no way to do all that work in just three hours. You and the other secretaries tried to console her. But when she asked whether Kendra meant no one could help, no one said anything. You knew she had meant it. But at the same time, you knew Kendra well enough to know she probably would not emerge from her office until the end of the day. She had blown up like this many times before and always seemed to hide in her office the rest of the day, perhaps out of embarrassment.

As Lashondra started in on the files, the others returned to their own work. You, however, just could not concentrate, feeling there must be some way to help. You had no pressing jobs that morning and were, in fact, well ahead of schedule. Indeed, you had been more or less just looking for something to do for the last two days. Shouldn't you pitch in and help Lashondra?

Pat Tyko saw you staring at Lashondra. "Don't do it. You know how Kendra is about people disobeying her orders. You'll never have any peace again if you help."

"But Pat, it wasn't fair. She didn't give Lashondra any chance to explain. And two minutes . . . two minutes! Give me a break!" you replied.

"Who said life, or Kendra, had to be fair? Remember last year when Neil tried to help me after one of Kendra's tirades? She practically bit his head off. Then, for a month, she made his life miserable until he quit. Are you up for job hunting?" Pat warned.

"She'll never know. She never comes out of her office after a blowup like this. If we each take one file . . . " You didn't get a chance to finish.

"No way!" was the response from the other three secretaries.

Lashondra was practically crying, as she begged, "Please. I need help. I need this job. I don't know why Kendra is so tough on me, but for two weeks she's given me a hard time. Maybe because we're both black and she is afraid people will think black women can't hack it in a big corporation. I don't know. But please, help me. This isn't fair. None of you could do all this work by yourself."

"Sorry. Can't do it. We need our jobs, too," Pat answered. The others agreed.

You did not reply yet, as you thought about your options. You felt sure you could help without Kendra finding out, unless one of the others told her. But the two of you still might not complete the work. Maybe you could talk to some manager higher up the ladder about Kendra and her temper. But that would not help now, would it? You could tell Lashondra to try her best and file a grievance if Kendra was not happy with the results. That would take weeks, though. And would Lashondra still be around to complete the procedure? Then there was the fact that Kendra was your boss and had issued direct orders not to help. She might construe your help as insubordination and go after your job.

Lashondra is a fellow worker and a friend. Although you do not know her well, you and she spent time together socially before she moved to your department. Part of the reason she requested a transfer was that you are working here. Surely you owe her something. What decision should you make to see that the situation is RESOLVEDD?

☐ 24. A Visit Home or Just Business?

IS IT ETHICAL TO PUT PERSONAL TRIPS ON YOUR EXPENSE ACCOUNT?

The brokerage firm that you work for in Chicago has a number of clients who live in Wisconsin, over 200 miles from your office. In fact, three of them are relatives of yours. Your grandfather, who had urged you to take the job at the brokerage firm, is one of them. Your uncle Louie and your sister Betty also do business through your firm.

Partly because of your grandfather's connections to your present company you had turned down another offer to accept the job there. When your boss discovered this fact, he asked you if you would be interested in handling your grandfather's account. You said you would but also would like to add your aunt and sister to your list of clients to prevent any family jealousy. The boss and the broker who handled their accounts agreed, so now you personally manage the investment portfolios of all three of your relatives.

For almost a year now you have conducted all your business with your relatives by phone. But it has occurred to you that there could be further advantages to doing some family business in person. While you were making arrangements to go home for Christmas and figuring all the costs involved, it dawned on you that if you also did some investment counseling with your relatives during your vacation the whole cost could be written off as a business trip.

The more you thought about it, the more attractive it became. The rental car would run close to $500 for the two weeks, not counting gas, insurance, or mileage. The after-Christmas ski trip you were planning would add another $500, not counting food and incidentals. But by merely taking your relatives' files with you, briefly making a few suggestions after Christmas dinner and while on your ski trip with your sister, the whole trip would cost you nothing. This would be a nice savings of at least $1,500 or so. Why not do it?

You do have some doubts about the ethics involved, although the whole thing seems perfectly legal. After all, you had been able to handle the relatively small accounts over the phone for over a year, so that personal counseling seems unnecessary. In fact, you are positive it is unnecessary. Moreover, none of your relatives had requested such one-to-one treatment. Your sister had even questioned the ethics of transferring her account to you, saying, "Isn't this like a doctor operating on his own family?" So she might have a problem with your plan. And grandfather is a really old-fashioned guy who values honesty highly. Would he believe you were being honest with your company by calling your Christmas vacation a business trip?

Then there is the problem created by the fact that what you are planning will be pretty transparent to your colleagues and superiors at the firm. Personal meetings are generally reserved for very large account holders, usually conducted only when the client requests them. None of this is true of these three accounts. Furthermore, you had never made such a trip and had handled these accounts quite easily over the phone in the past. Could you make a case for this "business" trip that your boss would believe? With a little ingenuity, you think you can, especially since he trusts your judgments about what best serves the client's interests.

However, it is a common practice to combine business with pleasure and write them both off as business expenses. You would technically not be violating any stated company policy nor doing anything illegal. Then, too, you would be saving $1,500. Who would be hurt? The company can afford $1,500. You haven't abused your expense account before, whereas you are sure your colleagues routinely write off personal expenses. But then again, it all seems so shady. Clearly, there are issues here you need to have RESOLVEDD before you schedule your trip.

❏ 25. Padding or Profit?

ARE YOU WILLING TO PAD A SALES PRICE?

This was your first business trip. Having worked as a sales trainee for six weeks, your supervisor felt it was time to send you along with one of the company's best salespeople to observe his handling of customers. Vince Collier was generally referred to in tones of respect and wonder at the office, he had been the company's number one sales rep for five years running. If you were ever going to learn the secrets of good sales techniques it would be on this trip with Vince.

On Sunday evening you met Vince at the airport and boarded the plane bound for Cincinnati. On the flight, Vince told you a little about his start in sales and for the company, while you told him how this was your first sales job and you wanted to learn whatever it took to be successful.

"A real go-getter, eh? Well, I can see that I've got a willing student here. Don't worry, kid, I'll show you the ropes," Vince said.

On Monday morning you accompanied Vince to two different companies and observed him in action. He was very good, but he told you these first two calls were the easy ones, since he had been dealing with these companies for years. The next call was where your education would begin. After many months of calling, Herb Norton of Apex Corporation had agreed to let Vince explain your company's product line. He had been happy with his previous suppliers, he'd said, but lately they had gotten a little hard to deal with, so he was looking around for new sources.

"Herb's a hard sell, but I think we can get him to throw some business our way," Vince told you as you entered Apex's front door.

Herb was a tough sell, all right. Every time it looked like he was going to agree to make a purchase, he'd pull back. However, Vince was up to the task and kept plugging away until it looked like this was it, Herb would sign a contract. But there was one more hitch.

"Look, Vince, I'll be honest," Herb began, "I had a pretty good deal going with my old suppliers until they had a big turnover last month."

"Well, you'll get a good deal from us," Vince answered.

"That remains to be seen. Suppose I lay it out for you? Your prices are a little high, though I believe you when you say the quality is worth the extra. But how about this? Suppose I agree to pay you 1 percent more than you're asking?" Herb leaned back in his chair to watch your expressions.

"Why would you do that, Herb?" Vince asked.

Herb asked Vince if you could be trusted, and Vince said you could. He explained that you were a real go-getter who was willing to do whatever it took to get a sale.

"Well, it would work like the deal I had with our previous suppliers. What I mean is, I'll authorize our company to pay the higher price, but you report the lower price to yours. We now have a 1 percent profit to play around with. You take half of that, I'll take half. I figure, with our volume we'll each make about $5,000 a year clear and free. Split with the kid any way you want. All you have to do is write up two order forms, one for my people with the higher price, one for yours with the lower. No one will know except us."

Vince said he'd like to think about the offer over night, and talk it over with you. After his last call tomorrow, he said he'd get back to Herb with the answer.

That night Vince and you discussed Herb's offer. You told him you were absolutely against it. But Vince said you ought to consider all the angles. He told you that this sort of thing was not all that uncommon, and it wouldn't hurt your company at all. You would be getting the right price for your materials, so the company would make its usual profit. Besides, a little extra cash would come in handy for both of you.

When you objected that the deal was illegal, Vince countered by saying there was no way anyone could find out, so there was nothing to worry about. Besides, you could always say it was Herb's scam and you didn't even know he was doing it. If Herb got caught you could always deny having written up two order forms, because they were typed and couldn't be traced back to either of you.

You continued to offer objections, but it seemed Vince had all the answers. He was a very good salesman, but you still had serious doubts.

"Look, we get paid to bring in sales. I bring in $400,000 of business every year, and our company loses nothing. You said you'd do anything it took to be successful. Well, did you mean it? I've had similar arrangements in the past, and it all worked out well for everyone." Vince continued on to say that everyone benefited. A 1 percent markup wouldn't hurt Herb's company, especially since your product was at least worth that much more.

You told Vince you'd let him know first thing in the morning as you went back to your room. Questions were running through your mind the whole night, Vince seemed to have covered them all, except the ethical ones. Sure, the economics seemed right, but honesty seemed worth more than money. You could just refuse to participate and let Vince and Herb do whatever they wanted. But shouldn't you report Vince to the company if you thought he was doing something wrong? Or should you just forget it, since Vince was so well respected and successful? It was obvious he'd done this sort of thing before. Maybe that was the key to success in sales. The company may have figured Vince was pulling things like this all along and really didn't care as long as he brought in the big contracts. Would you be seen as naive, a crybaby, jealous, disloyal, or not a team player if you reported Vince? This all had to be considered before morning while you RESOLVEDD the problem.

❑ 26. It's for His Own Good

PATERNALISM: VIOLATING AN EMPLOYEE'S WISHES FOR HIS OWN GOOD

You work in the personnel department of Amercord Corporation, a medium-sized company that recently provided its employees a new health care package. You serve as an intermediary between Amercord and the health care provider, currently informing the provider of the enrollment options chosen by Amercord employees. The employees were required to turn in their choices by noon today, leaving time for you to finish your tally and fax the information to the insurer by 5 P.M., as the companies had agreed. It was 11:15 A.M. when you came across an odd form filled out by a worker whose choice you thought you knew.

Winston Farquahar's form sat on the desk in front of you as you dialed the extension for his office. As the phone rang, you wondered what he had been thinking when he filled out the form. He had checked the box that said "REFUSE COMPANY POLICY." This was puzzling, since you had talked to Winston just three days ago and thought he had agreed with your recommendations. You had explained that it would be in his best interest to take company Plan B, which would provide him with the maximum dental program and a modified hospitalization plan covering 80 percent of his hospital costs. He had been skeptical about taking any of the new company plans and originally said that his wife's company policy and their own supplemental policy, which they paid for privately, were sufficient for their needs.

You know Winston fairly well, having played tennis with him on and off for two years. So you took a personal interest in showing that it would be best for him to take Plan B. You know he has three kids, all of whom have had major dental problems. He explained that he had taken out a private policy to help cover their dental bills and that he had paid close to $1,500 in premiums out of his own pocket. When he said he was happy with this dental coverage, you outlined Plan B in order to show him that payroll deductions totaling $350 a year would give him the same coverage he had now. He seemed to agree, and said he'd get the form to you after talking to his wife.

Winston's office phone had rung twelve times before you hung up and asked your secretary to locate Winston with the in-house pager. A few minutes later, he came in and reported that Winston had not replied. However, one of Winston's co-workers had answered his page, explaining that Winston had started his vacation that very day.

You called him at home, but received no answer. Then you contacted his co-worker. "Before he left, did Winston say anything to you about the health care form?" you ask.

"No, but I know he wasn't sure what he was going to do when I talked to him last week," was the answer.

"He didn't take any of the company policies. Do you know why?"

"Nope. He never said anything to me. But then, he's been very distracted while planning his vacation. You know, he's taking his wife back to Pennsylvania to visit her mother, who is seriously ill, possibly dying. He has been upset and rather unfocused lately. Maybe he just forgot to check the right box."

That must be right, you thought. After all, Plan B really is in his best interest, will save him money, and cover his family at least as well as his present policy. Furthermore, you recalled, the company wanted every worker to sign up for one of the three plans, as a high acceptance rate guaranteed lower company costs.

After lunch, you tried Winston at home one more time, still receiving no answer. You felt sure he had left for Pennsylvania. You felt even more sure that he had made a costly mistake on his acceptance form, which he would regret later. As a friend and as a company representative, you believed it would be in Winston's best interest if you checked Box B and signed him up for the company's insurance coverage. Even if you were wrong about his desires, moreover, you believed you would be doing him a favor saving him the $1,150 currently going for his supplemental coverage. You felt sure that, in the end, he would thank you for your help. The only hitch was your lack of actual permission.

The deadline is now just an hour away, and you still have to process ten more forms. You should be able to finish in time but cannot afford more time trying to reach Winston or deciding what to do. Once the forms are faxed to the insurance company and processed, there will be no opportunity to change any of the choices. There will be no coverage for individuals whose forms are not received today.

What should you do in the situation? Make a decision and analyze the case until RESOLVEDD.

☐ 27. Am I a Ghoul or a Reporter?
JOURNALISM, PRIVACY, AND THE PUBLIC'S RIGHT TO KNOW

You never thought that you would find the perfect summer job, but here it was! It was your first day as a summer intern at the local newspaper, the *Ripton Daily Centurion*. Ripton is a town of 12,000 people, located in the Midwest, and the *Centurion* has a readership of just over 15,000 in the three-county area. The *Centurion* is surely not the *Wall Street Journal*, but it is a good small-town paper with an excellent record of covering the news.

You have always been interested in journalism, but figured you would need a college degree to land a job as a reporter. Then, by chance, your uncle mentioned your interest in journalism to a golf partner, the editor of the *Daily Centurion*. He was interested, and arranged to talk with you. Two weeks later, having seen your high school records, received letters of recommendation from teachers, and interviewed you, the editor hired you for the summer. You thought this would be great background, useful when you enter college as a journalism major next fall.

Your first few days on the job were filled with the basic orientation: meeting people, learning how the paper was put together, and talking to reporters. Now you have been asked to accompany Carl Woodside as he develops the stories on his beat. You will work with Woodside for two weeks and then move on to other reporters who cover different areas. The editor explained that you would have an interesting summer, learning different kinds of news reporting, all of which would help you in journalism school.

For two days you have accompanied Woodside as he covered a political rally, a town council meeting, and interviewed three firefighters who had been injured in a gas station fire. None of this prepared you for the third day with Woodside.

While driving through town on this day, Woodside heard a loud crash, yelled, "Major accident!" and swung around to race back to the scene. There were three cars tangled in the middle of an intersection. Two of the drivers were just crawling out of their cars, very shaken and bruised, but not seriously injured. The driver of the third car was down on her knees, head in hands, crying and screaming. A quick look, and Woodside sent you back to the car for the camera.

When you returned, he pointed to the back seat of the car next to the woman. In it appeared to be an injured child, about 4 years old. The woman was apparently the child's mother. She was screaming over and over, "Call an ambulance!" A lady on the lawn of a nearby house yelled that she had done so. You were not prepared, however, for what happened next.

Woodside ordered you to poke your head into the car's open window and snap a picture of the injured child. The mother apparently overheard his instruction. She yelled, "Stay away from him, you ghoul! If you get near him, I'll kill you! Can't you just leave him alone!" At that, she rose and threw herself between you and the car.

Woodside yelled at you, too: "Get the picture! Get it now! What's your problem, can't you do your job? Snap the damn thing!" As he yelled this, he kept trying to pull the woman out of your way, asking her questions at the same time. "How did this happen? Whose fault was it?"

You just stood there, confused. As the ambulance arrived, Woodside told you to shoot the transfer of the child to the ambulance. At this point, you managed to carry out your orders. The ambulance whizzed away, and you spent an hour observing Woodside's questioning of the other drivers, witnesses, and police. Then you both headed back to the office to write up the story.

In the car on the way, Woodside lashed out at you. He said that your job was to follow his orders. As a journalist, you had to cover tough stories. The public had a right to see all the details of such a bad accident. Woodside went on and on, making related remarks.

When you protested that the woman had asked you not to take the pictures, Woodside screamed, "What does *she* care about the public's right to know? It isn't her job to cover the news. But it is ours. Next time, do what I say, or quit this job if you can't hack it, kid."

All the way back to the office and for the rest of the afternoon, you wondered whether you should quit. If reporting involved violating people's privacy, taking ghoulish pictures of injured kids over the protests of the parents, having to force yourself into the private lives of injured and emotionally distraught people, maybe you *should* quit. The whole incident struck you as horrendous. Does a reporter have only the obligation to get a story? Does it matter what the people in the story do or refuse to do? Is there some ethical limit to how far you should go in respecting people's rights when covering a story?

You have to decide what to do next. Quitting is one option. But it also occurs to you that Woodside is way out of line. How would the editor react if you go to him with your problem? Should you do that to Woodside? Maybe you should talk to some of the other reporters. Then again, what if they react like Woodside? How would that affect their relations with you, if you decide to stay? And how would the editor feel about your ability to do the job? Is journalism worth all this? Many questions must be RESOLVEDD before you can go on.

☐ 28. Job Insulation
HEALTH AND SAFETY ON THE JOB

You are being exposed to asbestos every day as a filing clerk at Mainline Construction Company. Mainline's office is located in an old, converted bank building. The files, with which you work every day, are located in two former bank vaults in the basement of the building. You recently discovered that the vault was lined with asbestos-impregnated wallboard and that the overhead pipes are insulated with asbestos.

As part of the yearly inspection of all businesses, a county inspector cited Mainline for various minor building violations last week. The most serious was the asbestos contamination in the vault. The county gave Mainline nineteen days to clean up the fallen asbestos fibers in the vaults. It also fined Mainline $1,200 for the violations. However, it did not require the company to remove or seal off the asbestos in the wallboard or on the pipes, although it strongly recommended doing so.

The company said that it had complied with the citation by cleaning up the fallen fibers. Beyond that, nothing was planned. A memo from the president's office stated that "Employees would be required to perform their normal job duties, including entering the vaults when necessary." The memo went on to note that no employees would be required to move any boxes or perform any activities that could damage the asbestos or release fibers into the air. It also stated that the county citation did not require the areas to be restricted.

You and the other clerks have been talking about the citation and the hazards of asbestos. The group is on the verge of demanding the removal of all the asbestos and backing up the demand by a walkout. You have serious reservations about whether this is a good idea.

One employee, 68-year-old Rich Potowski, vehemently opposed the walkout. In fact, he said that you were all nuts to be worried about this asbestos scare at all.

"You youngsters are all worrying about nothing. If you don't bother the asbestos, it won't bother you. Most of us old guys were educated in schools that used asbestos insulation. Every hot water pipe was covered with the stuff. I don't see any evidence of an epidemic of lung cancer in my old schoolmates," Rich argued, rather angrily.

"But what about all those lawsuits against companies like Johns-Manville? All those people with cancer who worked there?" you ask.

"Hey, listen, those people worked in very confined areas where the air was filled with asbestos so thick you could cut it with a knife. It's no wonder they got problems. We've wasted millions in this country on asbestos cleanup when the safest thing is just to leave it alone or cover it with a good-quality paint. You know, like in the vaults," was Rich's response.

You have heard, on the TV program "This Old House," that it is sometimes better and cheaper just to let the stuff sit. The real problems occur when it is moved and particles are released into the air.

"Look, the report said it was dangerous to let us into the vaults. That's the bottom line. Why are they forcing us to go in? I say we refuse," Lara Mayfield exclaims. "And Rich reminds me of those people who say that if it was OK for their fathers to beat them, it's OK for everyone. I just don't buy it."

"You know how much asbestos removal costs? I would guess about $12,000 for those two vaults downstairs. The company isn't going to do it unless the county makes it do so," is Rich's last remark as he walks out of the lunch room.

As it turns out, Rich is right. The company refuses to do more than the citation demands. This does not include removing the asbestos in the vaults. The president circulates another memo, restating his earlier one. It seems clear that you either have to continue to work in the vault or lose your job.

What should you do? Whose advice should you take? How can you best go about deciding the issue? Is the risk too great, or is Rich right? Analyze the case until it is RESOLVEDD.

☐ 29. Repair Quotas

WHEN YOUR JOB CONFLICTS WITH THE CUSTOMERS' BEST INTERESTS

As the repairs manager at a franchised but independently owned auto repair shop, you have been given a monthly volume quota by the owner of the shop. For each thirty-day period that you meet the quota, you are rewarded with a bonus that amounts to 20 percent of your monthly salary of $2,000. This is an important opportunity for you now that your two daughters have entered college. In addition, you tend to view it as a test of your skill, giving you a chance to exceed your base salary on a regular basis. The owner has made it clear, however, that if you fail to meet the quota for three consecutive months, he would consider hiring a new manager and either letting you go or demoting you to a lesser position with a smaller salary and no bonuses.

For the first four months of your job at the shop, there was no problem meeting the quota. Because it was summer and vacation season, many people brought in their cars for maintenance and repairs before leaving on their vacations. Now, in the middle of autumn, however, business has started to fall off, and you have barely made your quota for the last two months.

As business continues to decline, it becomes clear that you will have to sell the customers on repairs and parts that are desirable but not urgent. This troubles you, as candor and honesty have always been among your highest values. You are also concerned that losing your job or taking a cut in salary may force you to look for a new job in a very tight job market. There is also the possibility that you could be forced to ask your daughters to drop out of the colleges they attend and return home to attend the local community college.

Recently, even the mechanics have pressured you to "give the customers the old hard sell" so there would be more work. The mechanics want to put in some overtime, and have even been "coaching" you on how to encourage customers to spring for additional repairs "as a safety precaution." The mechanics also have mentioned that their livelihoods depend on you drumming up some business. Your conscience still bothers you, and so far you haven't tried very hard to sell optional repairs.

When you talk to the owner about your doubts, he says not to worry. After all, he explains, the repairs can be considered preventive maintenance that will save the customers money in the long run, as well as avoiding costly breakdowns with heavy towing fees. He reminds you that his quota policy is not negotiable and that failing to meet it will necessitate evaluating your future at his shop.

Your talks with other employees have convinced you that this policy is the creation of this shop owner. It is not part of the general policy of the corporation that sells the franchises. In addition, you are aware that the company retains considerable control over its franchises, although each is a privately owned shop. From what you gather, a call to the local company representative might get the company involved and lead to the elimination of the quotas or even the cancelation of the franchise. However, you are unsure of the company position on such issues and do not want to risk the boss's finding out about your meddling. If he found out, you might lose your job, whether you meet the quotas or not.

It would be safest to just go along with your boss's desires. Why not just look at it the way he suggested: as a way of getting the customers to buy preventive maintenance? Is it, after all, unethical to sell safety?

What are your options, and how should you handle the situation? You must decide, once you have RESOLVEDD the case.

☐ 30. Piecework or Peace?

CO-WORKERS DEMAND ANOTHER WORKER'S REMOVAL

You have been the union steward for the assembly area for six quiet months. But now trouble is brewing. Four weeks ago the company, an electrical supplies manufacturer, hired a number of college students for the summer. One of them, Paul Monroe, was assigned to your area, a diverse shop that completes seven different kinds of assemblies.

Paul began his job by working at a threading machine. His task was to center a metal cap and washer on the screw threads of an electrical conduit pipe, an insulating pipe through which wires are run. Then he was to hold the cap in place while pushing a pedal with his foot that started the threader turning, thus tightening the cap. It was a job that required practice and concentration.

Paul never came close to making the piece rate of 175 per hour. He just didn't have the manual dexterity to thread the caps quickly. During his first week at work, Paul never completed more than 75 pieces per hour. In the next two weeks, he worked his way up to about 125. Meanwhile, a number of the women who worked nearby took a liking to him, and tried to help him improve at his job. However, he just did not develop the skill needed to earn a bonus. But the women, all in their fifties, encouraged him, and treated him as if he were a family friend.

Paul seemed to feel at home in your department until you moved him to a new job during his fourth week. This job required little dexterity, but a good deal of muscle. He was to put a metal cover onto the body of a fuse box and pound the cover on a metal block to snap it into place. Paul, a weight lifter, was able to knock the cover into place with one hit. The four women who were doing the same job had to hit the cover three or four times to snap it into place. By the end of his first day, Paul was finishing over 250 fuse boxes an hour, 100 more than the hourly rate set by the management.

This was the source of the trouble. Piece rates were set by management in conjunction with the union. Every six months or so, a manager would come to observe a job, tally the number of pieces completed by three selected workers in an hour, then average their rates, which would then become the hourly standard. If too many people earned bonuses, or if one person worked significantly faster than anyone else, management would review the job and raise the standard rate to the number done by the fastest worker.

The rate for fuse boxes was 150 an hour. Paul's extraordinary productivity had caught the attention of a number of union workers. Two of them, Ruth Lahti included, complained to you that Paul was wrecking the rate. They were afraid that some manager would think that it was possible for everyone to do 250 boxes an hour and therefore raise the rate.

The women, Ruth especially, had always exceeded 175, thereby making a bonus that amounted to around $40 a week. If the rate went up to 250, they would no longer earn their bonuses. They demanded that you advise Paul to slow down his rate. They claimed that as their union steward it was your job to look out for the union members. The women pointed out that Paul was not union, because he was just summer help.

You told the women that you did not think it was fair to prevent Paul from earning a bonus. No one had worried when Paul couldn't make a bonus before. They responded coldly that they did not care, because he would be gone in another month and they would be stuck with the higher rate. You reassured the women by suggesting that they wait a few days to see if Paul might not slow down some on his own, fatigued by his fast pace.

You noticed, the next day, that none of the women would talk to Paul or sit next to him at lunch. Even Martha, who seemed previously to look out for Paul, stayed away. Paul looked confused and hurt by the situation.

That afternoon, you mentioned the problem to the union vice president, who agreed with the women. The VP simply said that Paul was not your concern, but that the raising of the piece rate was. It was unreasonable for you to expect women to work as quickly at that job as a nineteen-year-old, 210-pound male. He then told you to either slow Paul down or ask management to transfer him out of your area.

While reviewing the situation, a number of questions came to mind. Isn't Paul producing more for the company? Isn't that what everyone was supposed to be doing to increase profits? Weren't you all working for the same thing? Didn't Paul deserve to earn as much as he could honestly manage from his own hard work? After all, he wasn't doing anything wrong. In fact, he was doing too much right. Surely there is some way of addressing this issue that would be fair to Paul, the company, and the union workers. Then again, you were elected steward to carry out the wishes of the members. If you failed to do that, you could be voted out, forfeiting the extra pay the union gave you. You will need to consider very carefully the options and the values at stake in order to see that the situation is justly RESOLVEDD.

□ 31. Personal Beliefs, Public Policy
CAN A UNION FORCE A MEMBER TO SUPPORT ITS POLITICAL CAUSES?

You had been paying dues to the local union for almost five years when things changed for the worse, at least in your opinion. You were not a full member of the union but rather paid "compulsory agency fees" that allowed you to work at Cash Standard Motors (CSM), a manufacturer of small engines located near Burlington, Iowa. CSM operated according to an agreement with the union that sanctioned nonunion workers in certain areas of the plant as long as those workers contributed agency fees to the union.

The union position was that you and the other nonunion workers benefit from negotiations conducted by the union, receiving higher pay, more benefits, and better working conditions as a result. Therefore, the union reasoned, you and the others owe something to the union in return. Since CSM is not a closed shop, you were not forced to join the union. Your agency fees amounted to two-thirds of regular union dues, which are deducted from your paycheck in twelve monthly payments. For years you thought this was fair, because the union had secured for you all the benefits enjoyed by regular union members.

The problems began when the union, considered liberal in its political leanings, decided to put its influence and financial support behind candidates and organizations campaigning for abortion rights for women. The union subsidized a number of proabortion political candidates in the last election, as well as donating a significant amount of money to Planned Parenthood, a group known for its support of abortion rights. In addition, a number of union officials had spoken out publicly in favor of a woman's right to choose abortion up to the end of the second trimester, the legal cutoff point established by the U.S. Supreme Court's *Roe v. Wade* decision. You had responded last month by canceling payroll's authority to take your monthly deductions for union agency fees.

It isn't that you are opposed to unions or that you do not believe the union has a right to speak out on political or moral issues. Your problem is that, as a political conservative and a devout Catholic, you believe abortion is immoral and ought to be made illegal. As far as you are concerned, abortion is the unjustified taking of a human life for what usually amount to less than compelling reasons. You also agree with the Catholic church's official antiabortion position, which holds that having an abortion is a sin. As a result, you refuse to allow any money you pay to the union to be used to back causes and actions that you personally believe are immoral and unethical.

Originally, you had offered to pay your agency fees to a local charity that secures adoptive parents for unwanted babies. The union refused this offer but did suggest that you cut your agency fees by an amount proportionate to the percentage of its budget that goes to support prochoice causes. You had refused, saying that any money you paid to the union gave at least tacit support to its liberal stance on abortion.

Last week, CSM, with the agreement of the union, fired you on the grounds that the union-management agreement required all nonunion members to pay the appropriate agency fees. It would violate company policy and the union contract to let you keep your job. Management and the union agreed that your continued employment would amount to freeloading on the union. It would cost the company, the union, and union workers money that they had no obligation to provide. They would be supporting the costs of negotiation for you without appropriate compensation.

You, however, believe that this violates Title VII of the 1964 Civil Rights Act, which prohibits firing employees for their deeply held religious beliefs. Both CSM and the union deny that you are being fired for your beliefs. They argue, rather, that you are being fired for not paying your agency fees—a clear violation of the contract.

You would like to pursue the matter in court. However, a recent decision concerning a related case (*Employment Division v. Smith*, U.S. Supreme Court, 1990), is especially pertinent. In that case, the Court ruled that the First Amendment's clause guaranteeing the free exercise of religion does not apply to labor issues. In light of this decision, an attorney you consulted advised you that your case has little chance of success. Moreover, the legal fees alone are more than you will be able to handle, not to mention the resulting loss of time. You have no realistic chance of finding work elsewhere in Burlington and will probably have to relocate to find a job offering comparable work and pay.

With all this in mind, you have to decide what to do. What options are available? Should you take back your job under one of the conditions offered? Would this be an unfair compromise of your religious and moral beliefs? Would this be abandoning your right to exercise your own religion? What do you, in fact, owe to the union, and how important is this obligation? Just what is your obligation to your family in this case? Analyze the issue until it is Resolvedd.

☐ 32. ATV Dealer Encourages Use by Kids
DO YOU SELL A DANGEROUS PRODUCT TO A WILLING CUSTOMER?

All-terrain vehicles (ATVs) are rather squatty, big-wheeled, knobby-tired machines often seen in commercials roaring through the woods at high speeds, slashing across shallow streams, and climbing rugged hills. Such vehicles may have three or four wheels, and engines ranging from 50 to 500 cubic centimeters in size. They look like fun, don't they? According to some private consumer groups, they look like too much fun for kids to resist. The problem, such groups say, is that although these vehicles are built for adults who know how to use them correctly, dealers have been targeting children for sales.

In a recent national survey reported by the Ralph Nader-founded U.S. Public Interest Research Group (PIRG), almost half of the ATV dealers questioned said that ATVs designed for adults should not be used by children under the age of 16. However, about 75 percent of the dealers responding also agreed that children 10 years of age would have very little trouble mastering the operation of an ATV. A spokesperson for the PIRG asserted that ATV dealers are continuing to mislead consumers about the dangers of ATVs even after the adoption of an agreement between the dealers and the U.S. government.

The agreement, signed by Honda, Suzuki, Kawasaki, Yamaha, and Polaris—all makers of ATVs—in January 1988, bans the sales of three-wheeled vehicles in the United States. The agreement states that only vehicles smaller than 90 cc can be sold to children between the ages of 12 and 16. In addition, it limits the sales of larger four-wheeled ATVs to buyers 16 years of age and older. It is the responsibility of the manufacturers to notify the dealers and enforce the provisions of the agreement.

Of the dealers surveyed, 46 percent said that they would sell large four-wheel-drive ATVs knowing that children as young as 10 might be using them. This, however, would be a violation of the agreement. Furthermore, the telephone survey revealed that 99 percent of the dealers did not inform customers that the larger, adult-sized vehicles were inappropriate for use by a 10-year-old child. In fact, fifty of the dealers admitted that they would sell machines with engines between 90 and 149 cc knowing that they were intended for use by 10-year-olds. Indeed, eleven dealers said they would sell the larger, 150-cc, adult vehicles for use by the young children. A spokesperson for California PIRG stated that some dealers downplay the need for any special training in handling the larger machines. This also violates a part of the agreement, which calls for the manufacturers to supply free training and to add incentives for ATV purchasers and their families to take advantage of it.

The statistics compiled by the Consumer Product Safety Commission demonstrate that there is significant risk associated with use of ATVs, especially for children. In 1988, almost 40 percent of the death and injuries reported for ATVs involved children under the age of 16. There were 1,346 ATV deaths reported from 1982 to June 1989, and 36 for all of 1989. Of these, 20 involved four-wheel machines. Before 1985, a commission memo states, 156 people were reported killed in ATV accidents (11 four-wheel deaths), while in 1988 112 deaths were reported for four-wheel vehicles and 103 on three-wheel vehicles. Such statistics seem to indicate that vehicles are to be taken seriously, even by adults, and are not a kind of toy intended for young children, who may be less able to understand their dangers or know how to minimize them.

You have read two newspaper articles concerning such studies since your new job began at Marty's Cycle and ATV. In fact, you have talked them over with Todd and Larry, the other two college students who work part time at the store. Their attitude is "Don't worry, we've never had a 10-year-old come in to buy a cycle anyway." You have tended to agree and have not thought much about these problems.

On Tuesday morning, your fifth day on the job, a man comes in to look over your selection of ATVs. You introduce yourself and tell him you'll be happy to answer any questions he has about the 125-cc model, which interests him. After a few questions about speed, acceleration, and how easy the ATV is to operate, he says, "I'm sold! My kid's gonna love this thing. He's been asking about one for three weeks since he saw a commercial on TV, with the guys jumpin' the hills and the river. His eleventh birthday will be a big one, alright."

"He's eleven?" you ask.

"Not till next Friday. But what the heck, I might as well buy it today, right? He'll be able to handle it. He's a strong kid."

You hesitate, a puzzled look on your face. Marty, who's been listening to your sales pitch, steps over and says, "Right you are, sir! This baby's so easy to handle that a real baby could run it with no special training."

"Great! Well, wrap her up. I'll pay with my American Express."

"Ring it up," Marty says, pointing at you as he walks into the back room.

It is a $3,000 sale, for which you will receive a 5 percent commission. This is your second sale and your fifth day on a job that will provide your tuition in the fall. The money is exciting to you, and so is the sweet smell of success.

What should you do? Examine your options and the implications of each in light of your own knowledge and responsibility in the case. You must make a decision, once you have analyzed the case until it is RESOLVEDD.

❑ 33. Coffee, Tea, or the Sale?

A CLASH BETWEEN JAPANESE AND AMERICAN TREATMENT OF WOMEN

You have a reputation for efficiency, brilliance, and the ability to sell computers and business systems to the most reluctant corporate clients. As a result, you are the senior sales representative and vice president of Business Office Systems. You also have the reputation of being a pioneer for women's rights in the corporate world. You have fought discrimination for over twenty years on your way to the top. Now you may have to overlook some of your feminist principles while negotiating your first sale to a Japanese company.

You have done your research. You have studied the Japanese way of doing business, reading late into the night about the differences between the Japanese and U.S. corporate cultures. You know that during negotiations, Japanese body language differs from U.S. body language and that you must not misread the signals. Timing, etiquette, and cultural details differ. But you are set to do business in the Japanese way. The sale of a multimillion-dollar computer system to Oyakawa International Bank rides on your ability to convince the Japanese executives at today's meeting.

You also know, to your dismay, that women in executive positions in Japanese firms are not treated like their male counterparts. This bothered you, especially since one of the executives you will be dealing with is a woman. While doing your research, you have read a newspaper article that outlined the way in which women in Japanese businesses are treated.

According to the article, Japanese men expect that women will not put in the time and work necessary to succeed in the tough world of Japanese business. Moreover, female executives often serve as waitresses during business meetings! Yet none of this is taken as sexist, and a Japanese woman executive is quoted as saying, "It would be unthinkable to protest this treatment, especially when I'm on a career track." The fact is that only 1 percent of executives in Japan are women, although women make up 40 percent of the work force. The double standard in Japanese business is widely accepted, including dress codes at some companies that require all women employees, from filing clerks to vice presidents, to wear the same blue suits.

As the meeting began with the executives of Oyakawa International, you hoped that it would pass quickly, with no cultural conflicts. But it was not long before this began to look like a false hope. The Oyakawa negotiating team included two men and the woman, all three of roughly the same rank. These two men had considerably less experience than their female counterpart. The third man however, had higher rank than the others and considerably more experience.

About thirty minutes into the meeting, the senior officer said something in Japanese to Ms. Akiyama. She nodded, left, and returned about five minutes later with coffee and doughnuts for everyone present.

Despite your background reading and research, you are mildly shocked to see this happen but have tried not to let on. The negotiations proceeded smoothly for another forty minutes. You felt sure that Oyakawa Bank was going to buy the whole systems package you prepared.

At this point, the senior officer again addressed his female associate in Japanese. She nodded again, picked up the cups and papers from the doughnuts and left. In a few more minutes she returned, this time with pitchers of ice water and glasses from the cafeteria. She poured water for everyone and sat down.

You are uncomfortable with the way Ms. Akiyama is treated. In fact, Ms. Akiyama, who is probably more experienced in computers and purchasing than her male colleagues, from what you could tell from previous phone conversations, said and did very little. She seemed perfectly willing to let the men do the talking and was quite subservient to them. While the Oyakawa team conferred, you thought about saying something about their conduct before the meeting ended but do not want to insult them or lose the sale. What can you do?

Before you could decide, the senior officer of Oyakawa said to you, "We are very pleased with your proposal and would like to finalize this deal. Would you be so kind as to ask your boss to join our discussion?"

You were amazed! You have no boss! This whole plan is yours and your department's creation. It also seems clear that what the senior officer means is, "Could you call in your male boss, the person really in charge?" He hasn't said it, but it is clear he does not expect to close the deal with you, a woman. You think he probably does not realize what a breach of U.S. corporate culture had just occurred. He probably has no idea how insulting you found his request.

As you are about to say something in response, the senior officer adds, "And while you are looking for your boss, could you please bring us more of your excellent coffee? It has been a long day with too much talking, don't you think?"

This is it! Not only has he presumed that you could not possibly be the person in charge of this large a project, and not only has he constantly been sexist in his treatment of his female colleague, but now he expects you to cater to his wishes as well.

"Stop and take a deep breath. This is a multimillion-dollar sale," you think. How can you handle this in such a way as to protect your own dignity, but not insult your clients? Is that possible? Must you just meekly give in for the sake of the sale? Different cultures are one thing, but demeaning treatment is another. These are just some of the thoughts running through your head as you analyze this problem until it is RESOLVEDD.

☐ 34. Dictatorship of the Corporation

CAN A CORPORATION ORDER CUSTOMERS TO DESTROY A
COMPETITOR'S STOCK?

Your company, a middle-sized insurance agency, had just finished installing a completely new and sophisticated computer system. Being a computer analyst, you had been chosen to shop around for a software package that would match the new computer system in sophistication. The company's CEO wanted you to find the newest and best software, especially for spreadsheets. However, she also wanted to be sure that the software the company already had could be used with the new programs, because most employees were already familiar with the old software and would need time to learn the new programs.

You had met with software representatives from three major companies but felt that only the software from Pansy Corporation fit your needs. Their spreadsheet program, Pansy ABC, was simply the most sophisticated and best on the market. It made you wonder, though, because Pansy had recently slipped in the market from a 68 percent share to a 54 percent share. That seemed odd, given the quality of their programs. However, it might make their salesman, Gerald Chong, willing to give you a better deal.

Having already made up your mind to buy Pansy's software, you called Gerald to see what sort of a deal he'd be willing to give you. At first Gerald was very cooperative. He said the company was undertaking a very aggressive marketing strategy to try to recapture its lost share sales. Thus, he was able to offer you a 33 percent discount, since your old software was produced by MacroHard, a major competitor. This sounded very good to you.

However, Chong dropped a bombshell a moment later. The discount came with a hitch. You could only get the discount if you signed a pledge card that committed your company to destroy within ninety days all the MacroHard software you now used. Further, you were to pledge to use only Pansy software for a period of at least five years or the discount would be rescinded. Any new software you purchased from Pansy during the five years would come at its normal competitive price.

"Destroy all our old software!" you exclaimed. "That's something I can't promise. Our CEO wants to use the old software until everyone has time to learn yours. We can't retrain all our people in ninety days."

"Well, that's the package. It's a matter of our new competitive strategy." Gerald responded. "We can supply instructors to speed up the training. Besides, the price is good only for the next twenty-four hours. After that, you lose the 33 percent discount."

You told Chong you'd talk to your CEO, then call him back. Your CEO was surprised, to say the least. But after you fully briefed her on the capabilities of Pansy ABC and related software, she softened a bit. She did, however, say that all this sounded like corporate totalitarianism. She was reluctant to encourage such cut-throat marketing. Her final decision was to leave the choice up to you. But she insisted that you be sure that if you bought Pansy's package the training could be guaranteed within the ninety-day period. If you had any second thoughts, she said, go with your second choice, MacroHard.

When you talked to Gerald, he hedged a bit. He said that their trainers were excellent, but given the size of your company they might not be able to get everyone trained in ninety days. However, there was one more factor to consider. Pansy wanted someone to verify that all the MacroHard software had been destroyed and would pay you $4,000 if you chose to do it. He also said there would be a commission for you for every purchase of Pansy software in the next five years. Some quick mental calculations told you that this could add up to another $4,000 or more a year for you.

You told Chong you had to think it over tonight and would let him know your decision tomorrow first thing. This was a very tangled offer. There was the fact that Pansy had the best software on the market, and at a good price. Then again, there were no guarantees that everyone could be retrained within ninety days. However, chances were that even if this happened, you probably wouldn't be held responsible. If you were, you could probably shift the blame to Pansy's trainers. The extra money sounded good, but you had major ethical reservations about being a corporate spy for Pansy. Moreover, this whole marketing strategy seemed ethically questionable. Wasn't it a kind of corporate blackmail? Clearly, everyone had the right to make whatever legal contracts they wished, and this was not illegal, just a bit shady.

There is no easy answer. MacroHard software is not nearly as good as Pansy's, although your company had used it for years without any major problems, and could probably do so now. Don't you owe the company the best software available, however? But under these conditions? These are the questions you need to get RESOLVEDD by nine o'clock tomorrow or lose the big discount from Pansy.

☐ 35. Is What You See What You Get?

MISLEADING ADVERTISING AND A DEMANDING CUSTOMER

As the manager of the meat department at a large grocery store, one of your responsibilities is to handle customer complaints concerning your department. One afternoon you are called to one of the cashier's stations to answer a customer complaint.

Louise Shell, the 73-year-old customer, confronts you angrily as you arrive at the cash register. "This looks like deceptive advertising to me! What about you?" As she yells, she shoves a package of chicken breasts under your nose.

"I'm not sure what you mean," you answer.

"The sign on the freezer read, 'Manager's Special $1.79 each.' When I got up here, the cashier rang up $3.59. Now she refuses to give it to me at the advertised price."

You look at the package, which is marked $3.59. It contains two stuffed chicken breasts. The special was for $1.79 each, and you know that it means $1.79 for each breast, not each package. You explain this to the customer, who reacts in anger.

"Look, I tried one of your free samples of these stuffed chicken breasts yesterday. So I came back today and saw your sign. It said, '$1.79 each,' not 'each breast,' not 'apiece,' but 'each.' That means 'each package.'"

"But that was not the intent of the sign. I can see that it seems a little unclear, and I apologize. The price is for each breast, not each package," you explain.

"Yeah, and all the other packages were marked around $3, too, which I took to be the presale price. That's why I grabbed ten more sale packages. What are you doing, trying to make up for the lettuce sale by deceptive advertising?" is her reply.

"I assure you that was not our intent—"

At just this point the store manager, Sherri St. Clair, walks over and intervenes. She pulls you over to the side and asks for an explanation of the disagreement. After hearing your account of the problem, she orders you not to back down. You must charge the $3.59. "Otherwise everyone is going to come in here and try to pull the same scam. I've seen these senior citizens do this before. They intentionally misread the clearest signs, make a fuss, and then get some soft-hearted manager like you to give them the stuff for the price they want. Not this time," she says firmly.

"But Sherri, this is bad public relations. After all, it's just $1.79 and the sign is ambiguous. Wouldn't it be easier to give her the package for $1.79?" you ask.

"Easier yes, profitable, no. We can't sell those stuffed breasts for half price. We'd lose money. Heck, she's got about a dozen packages in there, too. We're not talking just $1.79. No, make her pay the full price or tell her to put the packages back," Sherri tells you. She then turns around and walks out to the parking lot. You realize that it is after 4 P.M. and she is probably going home for the day.

Your inclination is to give Louise the packages for what she is asking. But Sherri is your boss, and you should obey her orders. Moreover, Sherri is right. If everyone got the chicken at half price, the store would lose money. Then again, not everyone is asking for half price. Louise is just one senior citizen who misunderstood a sign. It seems like good public relations to give her the chicken for the lower price. But it is true that many seniors seem to make price mistakes that no one else ever does. Could this just be their way of trying to get a deal when they don't deserve one? You aren't sure.

"Hey, buster," Louise shouts, "You gonna give me these breasts for $1.79 like your boss just told you to, or you gonna try to take advantage of a little old lady? I've got a lot of friends who shop here that won't once I tell them about this ripoff!"

This shocks you. Louise obviously didn't hear your conversation. But everyone at the front of the store must have heard her. Now what do you do? Although Sherri ordered you to hold firm, no one will believe you now. Suppose you give in and Sherri finds out? You feel like telling Louise to shove off. But you know you must stay calm and try to get this problem RESOLVEDD. What is the best thing to do?

❑ 36. An Ethical Survey
SHOULD YOU FOLLOW THE LAW EVEN IF IT HARMS SOMEONE?

Citizen's Gas Company hired you and Felicia Alden, independent surveyors located in a nearby county, to map the property line between two farms. The reason for the survey, they said, was because they had to be sure who owned the land they needed to lay a new pipeline. The problem was that Mr. Mander, who owned one of the farms, had refused to give permission to lay the line on his property. Mrs. Kildare, a widow, said they could lay the line anywhere on her property, which adjoined Mr. Mander's.

This was good news for the Gas Company, as there was only a small slice of land that was geologically suitable for the pipeline. The slice of land ran almost right along the boundary between the two farms. It would cost the company a great deal of money to have to lay the pipe elsewhere, due to the fact that most of the county was situated on solid bedrock that began only a few feet under the fertile topsoil. Except for this small strip of land, under which was almost pure clay, there was no inexpensive place to put the pipe. Mr. Mander warned them that they'd better be sure where his property ended and Kildare's began, or else. Felicia and you had been hired to do just that.

After you obtained the appropriate maps and legal descriptions, the two of you headed out to the farms. As expected, when talking to Mr. Mander, he was very unpleasant, if not downright threatening. Neither of you cared a bit for him.

Mrs. Kildare, however, was as sweet as she could be, offered you lunch, and said to take as much time as you wanted on her property, then stop by for coffee and cake. During your visit to her house, you noticed that she seemed to be struggling to make ends meet, the furniture was old and worn, as were the rugs, and her clothes. She even remarked that if it weren't for her land, she'd be almost completely broke.

You both went to work plotting the boundary lines between the Mander and Kildare farms. After about an hour, you began to recheck all your findings against the maps and legal descriptions. There was a major problem. The legal descriptions and maps didn't match the fence line or the boundaries that Mrs. Kildare said marked her property. In fact, her property line was about twenty feet onto Mr. Mander's farm. There was an old fence there, but no matter how you rechecked all the figures, it was clear that Mr. Mander owned all the land the Gas Company was interested in. Moreover, Mrs. Kildare was going to lose a sizable chunk of real estate once the Gas Company filed the survey.

Felicia and you skipped the return visit with Mrs. Kildare and a week later turned in your report to the Gas Company. You received your check but went away feeling bad for Mrs. Kildare. But what could you do?—the legal boundaries were set. You were feeling guilty for not telling her but didn't have the heart to do it.

Six months later you had completed a job near Mrs. Kildare's farm and decided to stop in to express your concern over what the survey had shown. When she saw you at the door, Mrs. Kildare welcomed you as an old friend. Before you could say anything, she told you that the Gas Company had bought the rights to lay the pipeline on her property and for a very generous sum. She said the money was making a big difference to her.

On making a visit to the boundary area, you noticed that Citizen's Gas had installed the gas line as originally planned, for there were warning signs indicating the presence of an underground pipeline. Then you noticed that the old fence on Mr. Mander's property was exactly where it had been six months earlier. The markers ran right along the Kildare side of the fence, but you know they are well inside the Mander property. Citizen's Gas had apparently ignored your survey report and gone ahead with its original plans as if Mrs. Kildare owned the property. Apparently, it had not filed the survey with the county. Citizen's Gas was evidently disregarding both the truth and the law.

Knowing that you both have some professional responsibility as certified public surveyors, you and Alden wrote a letter to Citizen's Gas advising it of the apparent problem. You received no acknowledgment of your letter and saw no evidence that it had any effect. When Felicia called the gas company, she was put on hold for twenty minutes before being cut off. It seemed you were being completely ignored.

Now what? What should you do?

You have accurate and reliable knowledge of an ongoing violation of the law. You both have a professional ethical obligation not to be parties to fraud. To fail to pursue the problem might be a violation of professional ethics or the law.

Yet to take further action would harm all the wrong people. It would ultimately deprive poor Mrs. Kildare of much needed cash; give extra, unneeded support to the unpleasant Mr. Mander; and likely cost Citizen's Gas a pretty penny. Finally, it would ensure that you would not receive any further business from Citizen's and might well damage your reputations.

Is there any way out of this difficult situation? Analyze the case until you have RESOLVEDD the important issues, all things considered.

❑ 37. To Tell or Not?

ABORTION COUNSELING AND THE NEW "GAG" RULE

The Supreme Court has recently upheld a law that requires family planning clinics that counsel women on birth control and receive federal money to abstain from providing any information on abortion. In the state where you live, additional strict guidelines have been passed by the legislature dictating what a clinic may do when clients request information about abortion. The guidelines, as they now stand, instruct counselors at such clinics, when asked about abortion, to say, "I'm sorry, I cannot provide any information of that sort. Abortion is not considered an acceptable form of birth control."

You are a counselor at a private clinic that specializes in family planning but also provides full health care. The clinic receives federal grant money and treats many people whose health care is paid by federal dollars. The new legislation has restricted your options as a counselor and thus reduced your professional effectiveness. You resent the restriction on your professional judgment. However, you also respect the law and do not believe you ought to violate it. You certainly do not want any of your actions to jeopardize the clinic's license.

Last week, however, the director of the clinic, an internist with thirty-five years of experience in family practice, called a staff meeting. He explained that the first responsibility of all clinic employees is the well-being of the patients. He cited the codes of ethics of several health care professions to support his belief.

"Personally," he said, "I think the new laws violate our freedom of speech and destroy the doctor-patient relationship." He went on to explain that what a doctor told a patient is private and that the government has no business limiting the doctor's options for treatment. Such limitations endanger patients and, in effect, force the whole medical profession to commit malpractice. He concluded by advising the counselors to ignore the new legal restrictions and to counsel patients as they always had.

Immediately after the meeting, you discussed some of the issues with other members of the staff. Some of the counselors argued that there is a constitutional right to an abortion, as *Roe v. Wade* established and any legislation violating that right should be ignored. One member of the staff quoted Dr. Martin Luther King's statement that people have no duty to obey unjust laws. He then pointed out that depriving women of one of their legal rights by arbitrary legislation was certainly unjust. He urged everyone to perform an act of civil disobedience and to continue giving information about abortion to anyone who requested it.

Some other staff members, such as yourself, said that violating the law, even for the best interests of the patient, should not be done lightly. One man insisted that the fetus should also be considered a patient whose interests we must respect as well. Another staff member expressed fear that the clinic would lose its government funding, thus harming patients on welfare or those who couldn't otherwise pay for the clinic's services.

The discussion lasted for over an hour. When you left, you were aware that the director thought he could get private funding to cover the loss of government support. But you also realized that violation of the new restrictions would be against the law. How should you best handle the situation? What values are the most important to you as a professional counselor? Is obeying the new law consistent with the mission of the clinic? Is obeying it more important than the right to free speech, the right to an abortion, the right to informed consent, the right to advise honestly and openly, to practice one's profession in the patient's best interest, or the doctor-patient relationship itself? Analyze the case until it is RESOLVEDD.

☐ 38. Only She Knows for Sure
DID YOUR EMPLOYEE USE INSIDER INFORMATION?

Your brokerage has always enjoyed an excellent reputation both for its success and its honesty. In these days of Wall Street scandals, you have been as proud of this reputation for honesty as the company's monetary success. But now you are faced with a very difficult and potentially damaging situation.

As one of the senior account executives, you are aware of the seemingly unethical activities of your newest broker, Carol Sakawi. Carol joined your department four months earlier, having graduated with a master's in business administration from a top-flight eastern school and a bachelor's degree in finance from an equally prestigious college. Her references were excellent, although written by her professors, not other brokers. You were not worried, though, since she had done three years of internship with a top brokerage in another city. You had spoken on the phone to her supervisor there and had received confirmation of her abilities as a broker.

During her first four months, Carol had handled a number of new accounts well, earning substantial returns for your clients. However, you were troubled by her recent dealings as an assistant to another senior broker, Harvey Washington.

One of Harvey's accounts was a bank holding company that was rumored to be in financial trouble. Three weeks earlier you had asked Carol to work with Harvey to determine the truth of the rumors and decide what to do if they were. Carol looked into the sources of the rumors, while Harvey talked directly with the bank executives.

During the next week, the securities commissioner of your state suspended trading in the holding company's stock. This action followed a news story that reported a $12.1-million loss for the company that year, which their representatives had apparently kept hidden from Harvey.

To your dismay, you then discovered that Carol had been the high bidder for 5,000 shares of the holding company's stock. She had bid 20 cents a share at an auction for stock with a book value of $7, expecting the price to rise when trading resumed. There it was: Carol was now a stockholder in the troubled company whose problems she was supposed to cure. She was profiting from the company's failure. Was this a conflict of interest?

Carol claimed it was not. The stock auction was advertised in newspapers all over town, and she had not used any inside information. The auction was open to anyone, the stories of the company's problems were public knowledge, and she had not used any privileged information. In fact, she said, as far as the executives at the company had told her, there were no problems. Harvey confirmed the fact that Carol had been misled by the holding company's people just as he had been. But he also said that she was bright enough to figure out what was going on.

When you asked Carol if she thought she could continue to work on the account objectively, she said, "Of course." She insisted that her job in no way influenced her private investments and her private investments would not interfere with her job.

What about your company's reputation for honesty? Carol believed that would not be a problem, because she had been scrupulously honest and had not used insider information. That would be common knowledge in the industry.

"Sell your stock by the end of the day, Carol. Bring me verification that you've done it," you ordered.

Carol had stomped out of your office. "OK, she's upset, but she'll do it when she calms down," you thought.

Late that day Carol returned to inform you that she had decided not to sell her stock. Her private investments were legal, ethical, and her own business. If you disagreed, that was your problem.

Indeed, it *was* your problem. Your first reaction was "she has to be fired!" But you decided it would be better to think about it overnight and not react emotionally. Firing her seemed to be the only choice you had. But was it? Could you apply more pressure to get her to sell the stock? Could you just take her off the account and hope any rumors about her would not get past your office? But could you take that chance? If you fired her, would Carol raise a fuss that would be as damaging to the company as her questionable investments? As you rode home on the subway that evening, you wondered whether you would have the problem RESOLVEDD by nine o'clock tomorrow.

☐ 39. Is the Customer Always Right?

REACTING TO A CUSTOMER'S REQUEST TO REMOVE POLLUTION CONTROLS

You work as a mechanic in a suburban service station. You have just completed an estimate for a long list of relatively minor repairs to a four-year-old Pontiac. You have reviewed the list with the customer, Mr. Jackson, who seems satisfied with the estimate and ready to pay the $350 bill. Before telling you to go ahead, however, he makes a special request of you.

"Can you do me one small favor while you're fixing the other things?"

"I'll try," you respond.

"I understand that if the catalytic converter is disconnected, I could use leaded gasoline and probably get better gas mileage. Is that right?"

"Well, on most cars that's true. But you wouldn't save any money on gas. Around here, leaded is at least as high as unleaded. I wouldn't think about doing it to save money on gas."

"OK, but I would get better mileage, right? And the catalytic converter would never get any use, so I'd save money on repairs, wouldn't I?" the customer asks.

"Yes, but I can't disconnect it," you respond. "That's illegal. It would violate federal EPA standards, as well as state law."

"Come on, do me a favor. A friend told me that he had it done at the Argon station downtown, and they didn't give him any hassle. Besides, I can throw in an extra 10 bucks just for you. No one has to know. I'll never tell your boss."

"They may do it downtown, but I've never done it," you answer. But you know it is done all the time by mechanics on their own cars at home, and for friends. In fact, with a manual, a good home mechanic could do it alone.

"OK, how about 50 bucks?"

You hesitate, a little surprised by the offer.

"Look, I could just take my business elsewhere. I don't need to get all this dinky stuff done here. But why not make yourself some money and keep the $350 business for your boss? What's one catalytic converter more or less?"

You had never before been too concerned about the EPA laws, some of which you think are downright dumb, though others do seem necessary. Nor do you think that the lack of one catalytic converter is going to ruin the whole environment. You are concerned about fines, losing your job, and getting a reputation for doing this sort of thing, however. Of course, this job could probably be worked in while doing the other repairs, so no one would likely see you do it. Analyze the case, weighing the relevant personal and social issues until it is RESOLVEDD.

❑ 40. Is This a Trade Secret?
CONTRACTUAL OBLIGATIONS, TRADE SECRETS, AND A NEW JOB

You have been the director of personnel with Satyricon Industries for just six months. Satyricon is a banking consultant firm that specializes in straightening out the accounts of various types of firms. The job had gone well so far, but you now wondered if you were about to violate the terms of your previous employment contract.

You worked previously for Fellini & Sons Consulting, a firm almost identical to Satyricon, but larger and more successful. You had been hired as a personnel trainee, and given tuition to complete your master's degree in personnel management, subsequently working your way up to assistant director of personnel. In that position, using the skills acquired in graduate school, you devised a number of innovative personnel management techniques. These had helped Fellini to hire the right kinds of people necessary for their job openings. In addition, your employee profiles had been used to match Fellini's personnel with their customers. As a result, Fellini was able to assign the right people at the right time to suit the needs of their customers.

When Ben Cartwright of Satyricon contacted you about a new job, you had immediately notified your boss of the offer. She explained that Fellini valued your work highly but that further promotion would not be coming soon. She even suggested that you negotiate for the best deal from Satyricon and then inform her to give her a chance to match the offer.

As it turned out, Fellini could not guarantee you the same position or money that Satyricon offered. After lengthy discussions with your boss and the president of Fellini, you decided not to let this opportunity pass. Satyricon's significant potential for growth and your role in its growth would offer you a rosy future. In addition, the job would give you a chance to formulate important policies and use your talents to their utmost.

During your last two weeks at Fellini, your associates had been encouraging and wished you well. They even held a small party for you at your final personnel meeting. The next day, your boss invited you into her office for what she called a "farewell interview." She praised your work, offering to serve as a reference for you at any time in the future. She also wanted to refresh your memory about the terms of your contract at Fellini and the "separation clause." This included the provision that no employee leaving Fellini could use trade secrets if later employed by a competitor. You had signed an agreement to this effect years ago, fully understanding its implications. Your boss said that she was sure she could rely on your sense of honor not to violate the contract. You assured her that you would not.

It was exactly the "separation clause" that bothered you now. You had reached a point at Satyricon at which you needed to make some major changes in procedures. Until now, you had merely been cleaning up loose ends and sloppy procedures as well as trying to instill a greater sense of pride in Satyricon's work force. This had contributed to a small, but noticeable increase in their efficiency and profits. But now major changes were needed, and time had come for radical restructuring.

Your first reaction was to implement the strategies that had worked so well at Fellini. It was then that your conscience began to bother you. The strategies you developed at Fellini resulted from its support of your education and from major contributions by other Fellini colleagues. Furthermore, as far as you know, only Fellini is using the kinds of personnel techniques you had developed there. Did this constitute a set of trade secrets?

You had worked out a complete restructuring of Satyricon's personnel department and methods for matching employees to customers. However, you knew that 90 percent of what you had done was taken from your experience at Fellini. The "separation clause" bothered you. Would you be violating it by instituting these measures at Satyricon? If Fellini noticed Satyricon's increasing competitiveness and investigated, they would be sure to see what had happened. They might sue you for breach of contract and the divulging of trade secrets. The whole thing could cost you and Satyricon a great deal.

Yet you owe Satyricon your best effort and creativity. Without the help of the experience gained at Fellini, you would not be giving it. But can management expertise be considered a trade secret? How can you avoid violating your responsibilities to both Satyricon and Fellini? What should you do to see this conflict RESOLVEDD?

☐ 41. Profit or Loss of the Environment?
INSTALLING POLLUTION CONTROLS THAT ARE NOT LEGALLY REQUIRED

Your father and you had been discussing his latest idea for the family business, a small metal-plating company. He had just finished reading a series of articles on the environmental problems caused by various processes used in the plating industry. Because of the caustic and toxic chemicals used in these processes, the rivers and lakes near many plating plants are dying. Those which are still viable are in serious danger of becoming polluted past the point of easy recovery. Your father, the founder and president of the company, was troubled by these articles.

Your father wanted you to set up a study of the feasibility of installing a series of purification and pollution control devices that would treat the liquid wastes leaving your plant. He gave you a number of articles that describe such devices but that did not include details about their related costs. He told you to ask Claudia Bertrand and Juan Higueras, two plant engineers, to help prepare the reports. Finally, Paulette Kaye, your accountant, was to calculate the costs involved.

The task consumed most of your time for the next month. You and Juan visited a number of facilities that use similar devices but that are not in the plating industry. You obtained pollution figures from them, both before and after installation. Claudia studied the details of the devices and ways to apply them to the plating processes. It became clear that such procedures would be effective in reducing your output of pollutants.

One of Claudia's assistants, however, raised an interesting question. Why were you considering new pollution control equipment when the waste water you produce is well under the legal EPA requirements? Claudia had checked the figures and pointed out that you are meeting EPA guidelines for all the pollutants your plant discharges. The worst case was one where your plant discharges acid at the rate of 8 parts per million (ppm), while the EPA standard is 10 ppm. The other toxic wastes were even further below the EPA standards.

When you raised this question with your father, he handed you a number of reports and articles that cast doubt on the EPA standards. For acid, one report recommended no more than 4 ppm, saying that anything more is a significant hazard for fish and wildlife. Your father explained that he would like the entire plant to conform to the other levels recommended in the articles.

You took the articles to Claudia and Juan, recommending their standards. You also told Paulette to calculate the costs of reducing pollutants to the levels suggested in the articles.

After four weeks, your report was complete. The various purification devices seemed more efficient than even your father expected. All the toxic wastes produced by your plant could be cut down to the levels recommended in the articles.

The problem, of course, was the cost. Almost 40 percent of your profit margin would be eaten up by the costs of installation in the first year. After that, the costs of running and maintaining the equipment would significantly increase your production costs. To cover them, price increases or a smaller profit margin would be inevitable.

In an industry as competitive as plating, it could be disastrous to raise prices as much as you would need. No other plating companies are using the new purification devices. Most are meeting EPA standards, just like your company. So far as you know, however, not one is even close to the recommended levels outlined in the articles. So you would be competing with companies not hampered by the costs of purification devices.

When your father read the full report, he was pleased that the devices would greatly reduce your toxic wastes. He was troubled by prospects of reduced profits but said he would be more troubled by continuing to pollute at the current levels. He suggested that the company would receive some good public relations from making such an environmentally sound decision. And he thought the company could exploit that to its advantage.

As he looked over the figures Paulette prepared, he commented that he was sure you could remain viable and make about a 10 percent profit in prosperous years. During a recession, though, he admitted that you would have to hang on and swallow some losses once the purification devices were installed. All in all, he preferred to go ahead and install the devices. But he was willing to listen to any counterarguments you had. If you could convince him to leave well enough alone, he assured you, he would back you 100 percent, "After all, everything is legal as it is, so maybe you can convince me I'm being too demanding."

The decision is complicated. What is the price of a clear conscience? Do you have obligations that go beyond merely obeying the law? Should you do what will be most profitable for the company and its workers or not? Clearly, many questions have to be RESOLVEDD.

□ 42. No Cloaks and Daggers, Just Computers

PERSONAL VALUES, THE LAW, AND COMPUTER SPYING

You have heard of computer "snoops" who tap into various data banks to obtain helpful information. You are aware that much of this snooping does not violate any laws, despite its ethically dubious nature. You know that there is even an organization, with a code of ethics, called the Society of Computer Intelligence, formed by a concerned group of computer "spies." You also have heard rumors that, in the corporate world, French and Japanese firms are masters at obtaining information this way.

You have been working for over a year as a data systems specialist at Griggs Toy Company, which has about a hundred full-time employees. The company creates new toys and games, preferring to sell its ideas to larger companies such as Mattel, although it markets some of its own creations.

Until now, you never dreamed of becoming a computer spy. Last Monday morning the CEO of the firm, Darren Griggs, approached you with the idea of computer spying. He explained that the time had come to delve into various data banks containing information on rival toy companies. He explained that competition is getting very stiff and that recently foreign firms have been competing directly with U.S. firms all over the world. Any edge would help in the competitive toy business.

Griggs pointed out that Japanese companies have been gathering computer intelligence for years, and consider this a normal business practice. Since they think nothing special of it, he explained, neither should we. It is time to turn your expertise toward the gathering of information. Darren points out that the company subscribes to a large computer network database that compiles information of all sorts on toy companies and that he thought the firm could benefit from your searching the database for various bits of information about the financial status of your competition.

You hesitated at first, and Griggs reacted at once by stating that you would not be doing anything illegal. "We don't want you to illegally penetrate confidential information networks or bug corporate board rooms. We just want you to tap into the network for information freely given it by its subscribers. It's all legal."

You are still a little hesitant, given that your parents, devout Christians, raised you to be honest and to do unto others as you would have them do unto you, and this seemed a bit underhanded. But Darren has convinced you it's all legal and you would be only compiling freely given data.

During one of your information-gathering sessions, your computer blinks, the screen goes black, and then comes back on. As you check to be sure you haven't lost the information you were scanning, you notice a new list of numbers next to the names of companies on the screen. You realize that these are code numbers, exactly like the one you use to access the network. You also remember that Darren told you to be careful not to disclose your code. The code allows you to access your own data bank with the network, which contains confidential information the network will not release to any other subscribers.

At that moment Darren stops by and looks over your shoulder, immediately seeing what was on the screen. "Whoa, how'd you get those numbers?" he says. You explain what happened, and Darren grins and tells you to access those confidential files of the rival companies, as there are all sorts of information there that could really give you an edge in planning your new corporate budget. "This is some lucky break. We did nothing illegal, and fate hands us just what we need," Darren exclaims gleefully.

"What do you mean?" you ask. "How can that give us an edge?"

"Look, our confidential file contains our budget figures, including research and development. If we know how much our competitors are spending on R&D, we can raise or lower our own budget, increase our R&D efforts, and maybe hit the market first with some new products. Who knows what else we'd learn that would give us a leg up on them?"

You don't know what to say. These files are confidential, the network would never release such information, and you'd never want your rivals to have access to your confidential file. Yet isn't business a matter of out-competing the other companies? Besides, you got the numbers by accident. In the same position, your competition would check your files. And you have no legal obligation to keep their files private. Since this doesn't violate the law, many businesspeople would consider it justifiable. You've been handed a lucky break that gives you an advantage over the competition. It's no different from finding a confidential memo on the street.

You know this is true but still feel somehow compromised and dirty. What would your father and mother think? Yet many traditional Christian values are clearly inconsistent with modern corporate culture. How would it affect you to turn down this order? Should you even worry about such questions? Or should you just follow the order, accept the practice as legal and go ahead? These issues are not easily RESOLVEDD. But you must decide now, and live with the outcome.

Useful Ethical Values (Principles)

Moral Rules
- Principle of Honesty—*Do not deceive.*
- Principle of Harm—*Do not harm others.*
- Principle of Fidelity—*Keep promises and act faithfully.*
- Principle of Autonomy—*Permit and encourage others to act rationally.*
- Principle of Confidentiality—*Keep confidential information in proper circles.*
- Principle of Lawfulness—*Do not violate the law.*

Moral Rights
- Right to Know
- Right to Privacy
- Right to Free Expression
- Right to Due Process
- Right to Safety
- Right to Own Property
- Right to Make a Profit
- Rights of Future Generations

Justice
- *Procedural* justice provides fair chance for due process.
- *Compensatory* justice provides fair compensation for harm done.
- *Retributive* justice provides punishment received as deserved.
- *Distributive* justice provides fair distribution of benefits and burdens.

Distributive Justice in the Political Spectrum (from left to right)

According to:	the government should
• Socialism	fulfill basic needs of all, tax the rich to support the poor, limit power of the rich, regulate most aspects of society
• Liberalism	prevent starvation, provide equal opportunity and special help for those with special needs, reduce discrimination, tax some excess wealth of the wealthy, regulate many aspects of society
• Conservatism	provide equal opportunity, provide very little material support to the poor, prohibit discrimination, keep taxes low, regulate the economy to maintain free enterprise
• Libertarianism	eliminate all welfare, give no support to the poor, avoid discrimination, minimize government regulation in all areas of life